TRAINING MINISTRY TEAMS

TRAINING
MINISTRY
TEAMS

A Manual
for Elders
and Deacons

By Anne Stuckey

Foreword by Sven Eriksson

Faith & Life Resources

A division of Mennonite Publishing Network
Mennonite Church USA and
Mennonite Church Canada

Scottdale, Pennsylvania
Waterloo, Ontario

Library of Congress Cataloging-in-Publication Data

Stuckey, Anne, 1953-
     Training ministry teams : a manual for elders and deacons / by Anne
Stuckey.
          p. cm.
     Includes bibliographical references.
     ISBN 0-8361-9273-7 (pbk. : alk. paper)
     1. Elders (Church officers)—Mennonites. 2. Deacons—Mennonites.
3. Group ministry—Mennonites. 4. Mennonites—Government. I. Title.

BX8126.S78 2004
253'.088'2897—dc22
                                                                        2003027824

Training Ministry Teams: A Manual for Elders and Deacons
by Anne Stuckey
Copyright © 2004 by Faith & Life Resources, Scottdale, PA 15683.

Unless otherwise noted, Scripture text is from the *New Revised Standard
Version*, copyright 1989 by the Division of Christian Education of the National
Council of the Churches of Christ in the USA, and is used by permission.

International Standard Book Number: 0-8361-9273-7
Library of Congress Control Number: 2003027824
Printed in the United States of America

10 09 08 07 06 05 04   10 9 8 7 6 5 4 3 2 1

To order or request information, please call 1-800-245-7894.
Website: www.mph.org

*Dedicated to the
North American Mennonite Church
who heard my heart and made room.*

TABLE OF CONTENTS

FOREWORD

We tend to have warm, sentimental feelings about wonderful elders and deacons we have known. But what these people are supposed to do is often hazy. Such lack of clarity leads to conflicting expectations within churches and tends to discourage gifted folks from considering this call. This manual brings clarity.

Training Ministry Teams begins with the story of the elder/deacon in history, starting with the early church and how the first such leaders were chosen and what they were called to do. Then the vital role of elders and deacons in the life of the Mennonite church is outlined, from the time of early Anabaptists to the present. My response to this historical unfolding is a deepened appreciation for the vital role these persons have played in the life of our churches from the earliest days to the present.

The core value of this resource is found in the clear, easy-to-use sessions that address the vital skills-sets required for this ministry. Providing spiritual oversight, mediation conflict ministry, and crisis ministry are some of the most challenging things congregational leaders are called to do; very helpful training in these areas is provided.

Each session concludes with an "As You Go" section that contains group assignments designed to move participants from theory to action.

I was delighted to see in this manual helpful material on what I consider one of the most important aspects of this work—linking elders and deacons with the pastor as a mutually supportive team.

Putting into practice the calling and blessing of elders or dea-cons, as called for in session 3, will strengthen the support of the congregation and deepen the commitment of those called into this ministry.

Session 4 on "Working Together as a Ministry Team" contains the agenda needed to arrive at a common understanding of how to work together harmoniously and effectively. Maintaining appropriate boundaries and honoring confidentiality are some of the elements included in the covenant that elders and deacons are called to develop.

I recommend this manual as required reading for church lead-ers. It will provide basic and vital orientation on ministerial team leadership. It also is designed to be used as an in-service hand-book, a ready resource for training and equipping at your month-ly elder/deacon meeting.

I wish I had this manual during my years as a local pastor! I highly recommend this excellent resource for any pastors who seek to mobilize and empower their elders and deacons.

Sven Eriksson
Denominational Minister
Mennonite Church Canada

INTRODUCTION

The role of lay leaders in the congregation is more crucial today than ever before. Increasingly, deacons and elders are called to work together as a ministry team with pastors to provide spiritual leadership and discipling for the congregation. This kind of leadership is a responsibility that needs to be shared by many gifted persons.

A manual that focuses on the ministry of the deacons and elders is long overdue. In 1980, a Mennonite Church* study document called *Leadership and Authority in the Church* noted that moving in the direction of the New Testament pattern of leadership would include "finding ways for [deacons/]elders as well as pastors to have the appropriate experience, orientation, preparation and training to carry out their ministries" (23). This manual is the commencement of that mandate.

What Do Deacons and Elders Say They Need?

A survey filled out by deacons and elders from conferences across Mennonite Church USA indicates that most people called to such roles in congregational life have a relatively clear understanding of the role of the deacon/elder in congregational structure. Most also know to whom they are accountable in the congregation.

However, only a small number of these same people have opportunities for evaluation, and half of them receive no training for their ministry roles. Of the remaining deacons and elders, one-fourth say they received some training, and even fewer claim that what they have been taught is adequate for the task. Therefore, since deacons and elders seem to be clear as to the nature of the ministry roles required, it is not unreasonable to assume that they deserved to be equipped for the task.

The primary requests in the survey for additional training were most frequently in the areas of providing spiritual oversight for the congregation, mediating conflict, and partnering with the pastor in ministry. Second, requests for education were related to supporting the pastor, visiting someone in the hospital, or visiting someone in a crisis situation. And finally, deacons and elders seem least interested in receiving training for conducting meetings, visiting someone in their home or nursing home, and preaching. We can hope that these latter skills for ministry are ones with which most deacons or elders already are comfortable. It may also be that deacons and elders do not want to be instructed in such skills as preaching and then be required to do it.

This course for equipping deacons and elders responds directly to the call for ministry skills in spiritual oversight, mediating conflict, crisis visitation, and partnering with the pastor in ministry. Learning will be most effective if the entire ministry team, under the leadership of the pastor, works through the course together.

We will begin with some of the basics for all lay leadership groups in the congregation. Each group needs a job description and a covenant for working together. If the primary lay leadership group in the congregation is uncertain of their role and responsibilities, there will be conflict. If that same group has not developed an understanding of what it takes to work together as a team, again there likely will be conflict, and ministry will be completely ineffective.

Just as Paul told the Corinthians, "Since it is by God's mercy that we are engaged in this ministry," we cannot afford to spend our time in conflict or nonproductive meetings (2 Corinthians 4:1).

The Pastor as Teacher

Since only half of the deacons and elders surveyed say they received training, one can only assume that congregations currently are relying on these leaders' natural gifts or previous understandings in order to carry out ministry responsibilities.

This is wrong. Deacons and elders should not be expected simply to take hold of the ministry task without training. Such persons are chosen for their attitudes, interest, spiritual life, and calling. Ministry skills are learned and refined through the inner journey of experience and practice. Only when pastors reclaim the responsibility to utilize both action and reflection will learning take place in its fullest, deepest measure.

According to information forms received in one recent year at the ministerial leadership offices of Mennonite Church USA, a majority of pastors place a high priority on sharing leadership with lay persons and equipping members to release their spiritual gifts in lay ministries within and beyond the congregation. If equipping the laity is so important, then why are lay leaders not receiving the training they so desire? Perhaps this is a result of the movement toward a flat leadership structure that seeped into the Mennonite churches during the 1970s and 1980s. Also, the historically painful accusation of being guilty of the sins of pride and power continue to halt leaders, rather than simply keep them humble. Consequently, few pastors have seriously taken on the role of teacher.

In *Understanding Ministerial Leadership*, Marlin E. Miller highlights Ephesians 4, where equipping people is part of Paul's ministry. Far from discouraging others in ministry, the equipping ministry should "encourage them, nurture them, call them forth, mentor them" (63).

It is humbling to teach potential leaders. This kind of teaching does indeed take courage. But it is time for pastors to embrace the role of equipper and teacher without fear so the work of God's reign on this earth may move forward.

Education Means Inclusion

Every church has unwritten or unspoken rules about what is appropriate or expected. These rules can damage a congregation's health when new members are invited to be deacons or elders before they know the unwritten rules. Every deacon/elder group also has unwritten rules. Such groups can position a new person for failure by not disclosing tacit rules. This exclusionary behavior keeps persons who are new to the congregation or faith out of office.

One way of avoiding this exclusion is through education. Education trains lay leaders for their responsibilities and levels the ground for new persons, making the team cohesive. This makes success possible for the entire leadership team and limits failure for the most vulnerable members.

Format of the Sessions

When Jesus called the twelve disciples in Matthew 10:5-15, he did not just keep them by his side. Instead he sent them out to minister with power and authority and instructions. He told them where to minister and to whom. They were not to go to the Gentiles nor to the Samaritans, but to the lost sheep of Israel. He told them what to say and how to back up their words with actions. They were to proclaim the good news and then heal the sick. If they were not welcomed, they were to leave and move on.

In the same way, when deacon or elders are called to serve the congregation, they are given power and authority for ministry by virtue of their position. This is a spiritual calling directed toward a specific group of persons. Therefore, the first section of each session, "These Twelve Jesus Sent Out," includes a guided meditation and prayer time focusing on the topic for that session.

Elders and deacons, like the twelve, also need instructions before they go.

Therefore, the next section of every session, "Sent Out with Instructions," will reflect Jesus' method of training leaders. In this teaching part of the session, you will learn what you need in order to minister as a deacon or elder.

The third part of the session is called "As You Go," and will result in either a written job description, covenant, time line or practice in a specific ministry "as you go" proclaiming and healing in the congregation and community. These kinds of participatory activities help us take fuller advantage of what we've learned.

Also, you will note that I use the term *elder/deacon* or *deacon/elder* in each session. This is done to make the course reader friendly for congregations who use one term or the other. I am not advocating a new term. Since *A Mennonite Polity for Ministerial Leadership* uses the double term, I decided to follow suit. I have not used the term *lay minister* because I have insufficient experience in Mennonite Church Canada's congregational leadership needs.

Now is the time to truly utilize the vast gifts of lay persons in the congregation and call new leaders into ministry through appropriate leadership training.

* Several Mennonite groups recently went through a transformation process resulting in the formation of two new denominations, Mennonite Church Canada and Mennonite Church USA. Some documents cited in this manual refer to these two new entities. Other documents date back to the previous denominations, Mennonite Church and General Conference Mennonite Church. In identifying documents in this manual, original designations were retained.

Why Elders and Deacons?

A historical look at the importance of lay leaders

THESE TWELVE JESUS SENT OUT

At times the office of deacon or elder in any congregation may seem to be simply one more position to fill. We forget the honor that accompanied the calling of the first twelve disciples by Jesus himself. That same honor was accorded to the disciple chosen to fill Judas's place on the team. Read Acts 1:15-26. What in this passage tells you this office was important to the early church? How do you honor the office to which you have been called?

Pray that you will not diminish God's call to serve in this position but will honor God's work in you.

SENT OUT WITH INSTRUCTIONS

Spiritual Leadership in the Old Testament

Long before Jesus sent out his disciples with instructions for ministry, the people of God called lay leaders to provide structure to their corporate life. From the time of the tribes of Israel elders already existed. It is clear from the Old Testament that the title "elder" designated the head of a clan or a tribe (2 Samuel 19:11). However, we can surmise that there must have been many clans or tribes and therefore many elders in Israel; Moses was able to choose seventy persons out of the group of elders to go with Aaron, Moses, Nadab, and Abihu to worship the Lord (Exodus 24:1). Later, at God's instruction, Moses again chose seventy elders to help him lead the people when they were complaining about food. This time God's Spirit came upon those chosen so they could prophesy (Numbers 11:16, 24-25).

It is easy to see that the elders were quite powerful in this time period since they were the ones who made decisions for the tribe. For example, the elders made the decision to take the ark of the covenant from Shiloh into battle against the Philistines (1 Samuel 4:3). Again, it is the elders who demand that Samuel appoint a king for Israel (1 Samuel 8:4ff.). Even the kings were dependent on the goodwill of elders. King Saul pleaded with young Samuel to go back with him to Gilgal so he could worship the Lord, even after God had removed the kingship from Saul and given it to Samuel. Why did Saul ask Samuel to come back with him? Because Saul did not want to be dishonored before the elders of his people and before Israel (1 Samuel 15:26-31).

Spiritual Leadership in the New Testament

In the Jewish synagogue elders were appointed in a manner similar to the clan or tribal elder. In fact, the Jewish Sanhedrin we read about often in the New Testament during the time of Christ was composed of seventy-one elders. This group of religious leaders was closely patterned after the number that Moses chose to help him. It is this council that tried Christ in the house of the high priest, Caiaphas (Matthew 26:57). Joseph of Arimathea, who asked to bury Jesus' body after his crucifixion, also was a member of this council (Mark 15:43). Therefore, the tribal structure of appointing elders continued on into the synagogue and even later into the early church.

Spiritual Leadership in the Early Christian Church

In the earliest beginnings of the church, there were not yet institutionalized or precisely defined offices—especially in the house churches known to Paul. If we are looking to the New Testament to give us exact definitions of what an elder should do or be, we will be disappointed.

Even the terms used for elder in the New Testament are confusing. At times *elder (presbyter)* also is translated as bishop, overseer, or pastor. These terms are used interchangeably in the New Testament to designate ordained members of a plural leadership group within the congregation. Luke is the first to introduce the term *presbyter* to describe the men who exercised leadership in the Christian church at Jerusalem, using the Jewish synagogue pattern (Acts 11:29-30; 21:17-18). He also mentions elders from Ephesus in Acts 20:17. It is worth noting that elders were considered essential to the growth and maintenance of each new congregation. In Acts 14:23 Paul and Barnabas do not leave Lystra until they have appointed elders.

We notice the biggest change in church structure when we come to the pastoral epistles, especially Paul's writings to Timothy and Titus. By the time of Paul's letters, the charismatic structure of the early Pauline church (where offices were not described, but gifts were) had given way to an organized system of offices. In Paul's first letter to Timothy, the office of elder was assumed and is described as worthy of honor (1 Timothy 5:17-19; see also Titus 1:5). In summary, it appears as if elder is a broad term identifying the entire leadership group within each congregation in the early church. First Peter 5:1-2 exhorts "the elders among you to tend the flock of God that is in your charge." Here they are designated to care generally for the members and life of the church. However, within the elders group were those who were drawn out to preach and teach (1 Timothy 5:17) and those who would prophesy (1 Timothy 4:14), as well as those who were to manage (1 Timothy 3:4-5). There is an intentional division of labor among the leadership group, with not everybody doing everything at the same time.

The role of deacon in the Bible is considerably clearer than that of elder. However, it is not clear what the difference was between elders and deacons, who were chosen to distribute alms to the poor and widowed on behalf of the church (Acts 6:1-6). We know from James 5:14 that deacons or elders had a collegial way of working: "Are any among you sick? They should call for the elders of the church and have them pray over them, anointing them with oil in the name of the Lord." James calls on the elder group to perform this ministry together.

Spiritual Leadership among the Anabaptists

According to *A Mennonite Polity for Ministerial Leadership,* "There exists within our ... traditions two forms of ministerial leadership, both of which need to be claimed and reclaimed in the present time. Both forms [professional ministry and lay ministry] existed side by side from the very beginning of the Anabaptist Reformation" (69). Menno Simons defends the calling of deacons as having been taught by "Christ and his faithful messengers" in *The True Christian Faith c.1541.* In Section VII, "A Call to Repentance and True Faith," he laments, "No stone has remained upon another. All is desolate which Christ and his faithful messengers taught us of faith, love, baptism, supper, forgiveness, sin, repentance, regeneration, separation, teachers, deacons and true religion." This early Anabaptist leader seems to assume the office of deacon as normative in the New Testament church and worthy of being valued and not lost. Historians writing *Leadership and Authority in the Church* note that "by the middle of the sixteenth century, Mennonites had generally moved toward the threefold pattern of ministry; consisting of (1) bishops or elders, (2) preachers or ministers, (3) deacons. All of these people were usually ordained for life. They generally also carried out their ministry in one place" (8).

With this in mind, it is not surprising to read in the *Dordrecht Confession* of 1632 of three distinct offices within the Anabaptist church. Article IX indicates a high degree of commitment to the offices of the church, concluding that "without offices and ordinances the church cannot subsist in her growth, nor continue in building." Here the office of the deacon was part of a threefold ministry to the church of bishops, pastors, and leaders, based on the New Testament model of church instituted by the apostles. Interestingly, the *Dordrecht Confession* included deaconesses as one of the offices of the church. Not simply to be treated as unofficial deacons, deaconesses were to receive the same recognition/ordination as deacons. It says that the congregations "should ordain and choose honorable old widows to be deaconesses." In fact, the *Minister's Manual* (1998) reports that "the diaconate was the one office in the early church clearly offered to women. This practice is attested to in Mennonite sources from the seventeenth through the nineteenth centuries. At the end of the nineteenth century, Mennonites in Germany, Russia, and the United States reinstituted the women's diaconate as an order of celibate women with ministries in health care and education. As celibates, these communities died out, but individual women and men have continued to believe themselves called to celibate diaconal ministry" (9).

Over the next several centuries the Dutch church noticed a decline in the office of deacon as the professional minister took precedence. More recently, Harold S. Bender reflected on the place of the deacon in relationship to the development of pastoral leadership within the Mennonite Church. He noted that "by the mid 1900s, the office of deacon retreated in significance or [was] dropped when single, salaried, trained pastors became the norm in the mid-western states" (*Mennonite Encyclopedia,* vol. III, 704). By 1963 the confusing terminology for congregational leadership offices is reflected in the Mennonite Church's *Mennonite Confession of Faith*. Article 10 seems to imply that the bishop and pastoral office are synonymous: "The early church had regional overseers such as Timothy, and bishops (pastors) and deacons in local congregations." However, the threefold ministry still seems to exist, including the overseer, bishop/pastor, and deacon.

A change in leadership titles again is reflected in *Leadership and Authority in the Church*. This 1980 document articulates the trend to dismiss the office of deacons ordained for life within the Mennonite Church tradition. It states that from the 1950s and

1960s there had been a tendency to drop the office of ordained deacons and to move in the direction of a one-pastor form of leadership with a board of elders or church council. In Mennonite Church congregations, the single pastor pattern usually has been combined with the development of a group of lay leaders in the form of a church council or an elder board. The lay leaders generally are elected for a limited period of time and rarely ordained. In the General Conference Mennonite Church, the role of the deacon continued throughout this time, although by now the *Aeltester* or elder/bishop was being replaced by a Conference Minister.

The most noticeable change regarding the office of deacon in the Mennonite Church seemed to reflect the North American embrace of flat leadership structures of the 1970s. In *Congregations and Their Servant Leaders*, Harold Bauman acknowledges that the names of the offices are many and varied, including bishops, ministers, pastors, and elders. However, in this document Bauman calls all these offices "elders." In addition, he suggests that there are overseers, deacons, and stewards. Bauman says it is difficult to base the threefold ministry (bishop, minister, deacon) on the New Testament as the result of careful word study. This statement alone is a drastic change from Anabaptist church traditional reading of the New Testament.

While the Mennonite Church rapidly was discarding the office of deacon, another *Minister's Manual* published in 1983 by two General Conference pastors, Heinz Janzen and Dorothea Janzen, included a service for the installation of a deacon. In this manual, the ministry is designated as the "office of deacon/elder," which tries to include both Mennonite Church and General Conference Mennonite Church realities. The joint General Conference Mennonite Church and Mennonite Church *Confession of Faith in a Mennonite Perspective* adopted in 1995 accurately reflected the multiple titles currently in use for the office of the deacon. Article 15 reads, "The church calls, trains, and appoints gifted men and women to a variety of leadership ministries on its behalf. These may include such offices as pastor, deacon and elder" (59). This joint church statement continues to hold both the *deacon* and *elder* terminology.

Almost as if coming full circle back to the beginning of Anabaptist congregational structure, *A Mennonite Polity for Ministerial Leadership*, published in 1996, returns significantly to the threefold ministry characteristic of most of Anabaptist history, recognizing three offices of ministry:

1. Oversight Ministries
2. Pastoral Ministries
3. Elder/Deacon Ministries

Of elder/deacon ministries, it says: "The lay ministry (the ministry of unordained members) is that form which emerges out of the congregation through the affirmation of gifts, ... often requires another vocation, and thus is a position with a part-time commitment and often alongside a professional pastor.... Today, we cannot and should not value one more highly than the other; both professional and lay ministry need to be seen as valid and valued forms of ministerial leadership. We most want to see them as two forms which complement each other and work together in harmony so as to contribute to the well-being and harmony of the church" (70-71).

With the exception of church statements published in the early 1980s reflecting the social milieu of the sixties and seventies, most other references point to the office of the deacon as part of a three-fold ministry pattern. This consistency is amazing, considering that these church statements reflect a variety of geographic locations from Europe through North America and span almost 475 years. The noticeable leveling of leadership positions to make all leaders equal in Bauman's *Congregations and Their Servant Leaders* indicates the antihierarchical mood of the 1960s and 1970s in the United States and Canada. However, church statements from the 1990s again have returned to the language of a specific office when speaking of the elder/deacon lay leadership position in the congregation.

As You Go

Draw a time line showing when elders or deacons were introduced to your congregational structure.

- If women are part of the elder/deacon group, when was the first one chosen?

- When was the first church council instated?

- Did the work of the church council change the role of the elders or deacons? If there is no church council, how does that affect the work of the elders/deacons?

What Do Deacons and Elders Do?

Answers from Anabaptist theology

THESE TWELVE JESUS SENT OUT

Stephen was likely the consummate deacon. Read Acts 6:1-10. According to Luke, Stephen was chosen along with Philip, Prochorus, Nicanor, Timon, Parmenas, and Nicolaus to serve the daily distribution of food to the widows. But we also are told that Stephen did great wonders and signs and was a wise, Spirit-filled preacher. That is a broad range of gifts to use in his ministry as a deacon. What gifts do you bring to the ministry of the deacon/elder?

Pray you will have the grace to use all the gifts you have been given for this ministry.

SENT OUT WITH INSTRUCTIONS

Biblical Tasks of Elders and Deacons

Deacons and elders initially were given a rather specific task in the New Testament. They were chosen because the apostles needed help caring for the Greek widows and orphans who were not

24

receiving what they needed in the daily distribution of food. Since the apostles recognized they could not do everything, they designated deacons to pick up the responsibility of waiting on tables (Acts 6:1-4). However, we find deacons/elders named for their involvement in other ministries as well. James instructs them to anoint and pray for the sick (James 5:14).

Leadership and the Anabaptists

When asked what deacons or elders do in the congregation today, many people have a general idea but find it difficult to articulate specifically the role and task of these lay leaders. Most know this group traditionally has been given authority to provide some form of oversight for the congregation but are not clear how extensive the scope of that oversight is. Do the elders supervise the choice of Sunday school materials? Do deacons make sure trustees complete their work so the roof doesn't leak? Is it this group that oversees the work of the pastor? The current ambiguity surrounding these questions leads one to ask whether there is a time-worn job description for deacons and elders.

In reality, a chronological sampling of historical confessions of faith, polity statements, and other church documents from the Mennonite tradition can provide us with considerable insight. Many church statements are explicit about the specific ministries required of the deacon's office, including tasks from church discipline to preaching. Therefore, we can find some distinct commonalities among the traditional statements of the church. In the following excerpts we will see how the role of the deacon/elder changed little from the 1500s until the 1950s-60s.

Instruction on Excommunication (1558)

In this first teaching tool, Menno Simons gives deacons considerable power to be involved in church discipline. "Finally I entreat all elders, teachers, ministers and deacons in the love of Christ, not to teach this whole difficult matter recklessly, sternly, and unwisely, but in full fear of God and with Christian prudence and paternal care" (Complete Writings of Menno Simons, 974). It may be sobering to learn that the earliest Anabaptist documents cite church discipline as a primary task of the deacons. That probably would not be the calling of choice for most deacons or elders today. Discipline was not the primary concern of the earliest deacons in Acts 6:1-6. Instead, they initially were called to care for widows who were being neglected. Care for widows is assumed by Menno Simons; he adds discipline as an additional responsibility. Most of the following statements would align themselves closely with the New Testament model.

Concept of Cologne (1591)

Written only thirty-three years after Menno Simons' statement on the responsibility of deacons to carry out church discipline, the *Concept of Cologne* reflects the role traditionally given to deacons. It says, "Deacons shall be . . . assigned the care of the poor. They are to distribute to the poor the gifts received for this purpose, so that the giver shall remain unknown as Christ teaches" (*Mennonite Encyclopedia*, vol. I, 663). The care of the poor through the collection and disbursement of the alms fund is the focus of this statement. However, it should not be lost that the deacon was called to carry out this ministry in a confidential manner so as not to expose those giving the money.

Dordrecht Confession (1632)

Another ministry is added to the role of the deacon in the *Dordrecht Confession*. Article IX begins as we would expect, stating that in order to look after and care for the poor "deacons may receive the contributions and alms [from the congregation] in order to dispense them faithfully and with all propriety to the poor and needy saints." However, it continues that "for the assistance and relief of the elders, [deacons] may exhort the church and labor also in the Word and in teaching." In this case, "elders" is the title given to those ministers given the responsibility for preaching. Here, deacons are instructed to assume the preaching and teaching in the congregation when ministers or elders need relief.

Another change is the inclusion of deaconesses in the ministry traditionally given to deacons. This confession says that, along with the deacons, deaconesses "should visit, comfort, and care for the poor, weak, ill, distressed and needy people, as also widows and orphans and help to alleviate the needs of the congregation to the best of their abilities" (*Introduction to Theology*, 380). It is clear that both deacons and deaconesses were called to look after the poor, the sick, and the afflicted. The congregation also was instructed to choose deacons who could preach if necessary. This ministry does not seem to be extended to the deaconesses.

The *Concept of Cologne* brought the High German, Frisian, and later the Waterlander congregations into agreement. However, it wasn't until the *Dordrecht Confession* came into being that this widely accepted statement joined the former groups with more conservative Mennonite groups. In 1660 the Palatinate and Alsatian churches adopted the *Dordrecht Confession* and brought it to America. From this we can assume there was growing congruence among the various Mennonite groups regarding the appropriate role for deacons and that such an understanding came to America with the earliest immigrants in 1683.

The Ris Confession (Mennonite Articles of Faith, 1766)

In the General Conference Mennonite tradition, responsibilities of deacons were clearly outlined in Article XXIV of the *Ris Confession of Faith*. It says, "The deacons have likewise and in many points similar [to overseer] holy responsibilities. 1 Timothy 3:8-13. They must help to rule the church in the fear of God (1 Timothy 5:17), collect the useful offerings, exercise faithful stewardship with these, and whatever other gifts there may be, and according to need distribute in the best way, impartially, with kindness and love. 2 Corinthians 8:19-21; 9:5-14" (*One Lord, One Church*, 95).

West Prussian Confession (1895)

Mennonites from eastern regions held similar views of the role of the deacon. "We also hold fast to the Apostolic arrangement according to which, along side of preachers, deacons or alms-keepers are maintained in the church, who support the poor through the alms which are given by generous hearts, supply the wants of needy members, practice mercy with gladness and otherwise lend a helping hand in the church in order that it may be well administered" (*Mennonite Encyclopedia*, vol. I, 684; vol. II, 22). Again, the care of the poor and ministering to the needs of church members is the primary task of the deacon. It is interesting to note, however, that deacons also are asked to provide general care or oversight of the congregation so that it functions effectively. Until now this responsibility may have fallen to the deacons, but it had not explicitly been stated as such.

Mennonite Encyclopedia (1957)

According to Harold S. Bender in 1957, the work of the deacon was outlined as:

1. Service to the poor and needy members, usually including administration of the poor fund or alms monies.
2. Assisting the pastor or bishop in the administration of the ordinances of baptism and communion (the deacon usually provides the bread and wine or grape juice, as well as providing the arrangements for foot washing).
3. Assisting the bishop or pastor in visiting the sick and erring members, as well as helping to overcome or arbitrate difficulties between members, serving on the ministerial council of the congregation in matters of church activities and discipline.
4. Reading the opening Scripture lesson and offering the opening prayer at the regular worship services as may be directed by the minister in charge, and having charge of the entire service in the absence of the minister (*Mennonite Encyclopedia*, vol. II, 22).

Again, the role of the deacon sounds somewhat familiar in the areas of caring for the poor and assisting in matters of church discipline, especially in times of conflict. New additions by the 1950s included more detailed requirements for the deacon's involvement in such practices of the church as communion and foot washing.

The deacons were to ready the bread and wine or grape juice for serving and prepare basins and towels for foot washing. Increased responsibilities for worship leading also appear in this description of the role of the deacon. By 1957 the role of the deacon was growing rather than diminishing, but that soon was to change.

Mennonite Confession of Faith (1963)

Only six years after Bender wrote the most detailed job description for deacons to date, the *Mennonite Confession of Faith* gives us clues that the role of the deacon was not nearly as clear as Bender outlined. For example, Article 10 declares with little other explanation that the deacon's work was simply to help the pastors. It says, "The early church had regional overseers such as Timothy, and bishops (pastors) and deacons in local congregations. Upon the pastors lay the responsibility for the leadership and pastoral care of the congregations, and the deacons served as their helpers." This rather broad description stands in sharp contrast to Bender's four points. Not only was the Mennonite church changing due to resistance expressed against the previous power of bishops, but the impact of societal attitudes toward leadership in general also was taking effect.

Leadership and Authority in the Church (1980)

Due to the gradual confusion regarding the role of leadership in the congregation, a study document was created for the Mennonite General Assembly in 1980. In reviewing the history of the role of the deacon, this document states that in the twentieth century "deacons have historically fulfilled many tasks. Their duties usually include caring for the poor of the congregation, assisting the bishop in the administration of the ordinances and in discipline, reading scripture in worship services, and assisting bishops and preachers in visiting the sick." This summary rings true with the statements of faith we already have surveyed. But the description of the current role of the deacon is what is most surprising (9).

The change from *deacon* to *elder* terminology stands out in this document. After the historical review, the term *deacon* almost totally disappears from this document. However, not only the terminology changes. The overall picture of the role of the elder is significantly altered from the deacon of the past. Now we are told: "The elders may function in ways which give general oversight and direction to congregational life usually in administrative and organizational matters and rarely in preaching, teaching and pastoral visitation" (23). The move away from ministry toward more administrative functions cannot be minimized. This trend was more prevalent in the Mennonite Church than in the General Conference Mennonite Church. In General Conference congregations, generally the historical role of the deacon, as well as the terminology, remained intact. This was reflected in the *Minister's Manual* of 1983.

Minister's Manual (1983)

The *Minister's Manual* was written to serve both General Conference and Mennonite Church ministers. Therefore, it reflects a historical understanding of the role of the deacon or elder. It says, "In our Mennonite tradition deacons have been called to serve the poor and needy, to visit the sick, to assist the pastor with baptism and communion, to provide spiritual leadership in the church, and to arbitrate in difficulties between members" (64). Even though this explanation of the deacon role is in line with past understandings, it often did not mirror current realities in the Mennonite Church.

Called to Caregiving (1987)

Church of the Brethren, Mennonite Brethren, General Conference Mennonite, and Mennonite churches published a resource for equipping deacons in 1987. In it Erland Waltner noted the change in the ministry and status of the deacon: "In both Church of the Brethren and Mennonite congregations the role of the deacon in recent years has experienced change in nature and in status. In the late nineteenth century and the first four decades of this century, the office of the deacon wielded much power in many congregations. Part of this influence was due to the annual diaconal visit which could result in the disciplining of members and their exclusion from communion services. When the deacon visit became too anxiety-producing, congregations began to drop the practice; and this in turn lessened both the responsibilities and the authority of deacons" (31). It is obvious that the disciplinary role of the deacon was quite important up to this time, and its loss caused a major change.

Ordinal (1987)

The General Conference Mennonite Church's Committee on the Ministry wrote a document called the *Ordinal* to bring some unity of understanding to the structure of leadership in the church. Its brief statement on the role of the deacon claims that "deacons have generally been a lay group who serve the church with and in support of the pastor" (16). Further explanation about what is meant by serving the church or supporting the pastor was not included, but one can assume that previous understandings of the specific duties of the deacon were still in effect at that time.

Confession of Faith in a Mennonite Perspective (1995)

In a similar vein this first joint confession of faith adopted by the Mennonite Church and the General Conference Mennonite Church adds little to our understanding of the responsibilities of deacons and elders. Article 15, titled "Ministry and Leadership," identifies no specific ministry for deacons and elders.

A Mennonite Polity for Ministerial Leadership (1996)

However, *A Mennonite Polity for Ministerial Leadership* gives excellent instruction for deacons and elders. It declares that these leaders are chosen "to do pastoral care with the pastor, creating a ministerial leadership team, providing spiritual oversight of the congregation, and serving as a support group for the pastor. They may do pastoral care, preach, look after the needy and provide encouragement and support for the pastor" (78-79). Here we see a more complete design for the ministry conducted by deacons or elders than since Harold Bender's contribution in 1957. Included is caring for the poor, preaching the Word, supporting the pastor, and providing pastoral care. Noticeably missing is the responsibility for church discipline, unless one considers that a form of pastoral care. Supporting the pastor with encouragement and counsel has been given added significance. This language is considerably different than merely assisting the pastor, as it was described in the past.

Minister's Manual (1998)

The most recent *Minister's Manual* continues many of the previous historical understandings, including providing for the poor and dealing with conflict, though it is not called church discipline here. It says, "From the early church onward through the Reformation, deacons were assigned both practical duties of overseeing ministry to the poor and disadvantaged within and beyond the congregation, and the spiritual task of taking initiative to heal misunderstanding and strife in the congregation" (175).

Summary

From all we have read, it is safe to say that deacons and elders have a long history of caring for the poor, distributing the alms fund, visitation, providing pastoral services in the absence of the pastor, and being involved in church discipline. In fact, this description has been used with only a few variations throughout the entire history of the Anabaptist/Mennonite church. Only since the 1950s and 1960s, with the move to an elder board in the Mennonite Church and its heavier emphasis on congregational oversight, including administration, have many of the ministry aspects of the deacon's role changed. This is most evident in the document, *Leadership and Authority in the Church*.

It remains to be seen how the role of deacon/elder will change in the future. We still have in our congregations the poor, widows and widowers, those in conflict, and those needing visitation. But it is increasingly difficult to find lay leaders who are willing to give their time to these ministries. The trend toward more involvement in administration grows, since it is easier to meet and make decisions for the pastor to carry out than to be directly involved in ministry.

As You Go

1. List all the tasks for which the deacon/elder board of your congregation is currently responsible.

2. Divide your list into these categories: Caring for the Needy, Pastoral Care and Visitation, Managing Conflict, Supporting the Pastor(s), Leadership in Worship, Administration, Spiritual Care of the Congregation, Other. Which category requires most of your meeting time?

3. If you have a job description, how well does it reflect your current responsibilities? Does it reflect well your spiritual priorities? This review should occur on an annual basis when new deacons or elders begin their ministry.

4. A job description is crucial to knowing what you have been called to do as deacons or elders. It is also crucial in helping the congregation know whom to call to this ministry, especially in assessing the gifts of newer members. Many newer members may be gifted for this ministry but never are invited to consider it because the expectations for deacons or elders often go unstated.

If you do not have a job description, use the form outlined in Appendix A to write what your congregation is calling you to do. It is wise to have the deacons and elders sign and date this document on a yearly basis.

Calling and Blessing Lay Leaders for Ministry

THESE TWELVE JESUS SENT OUT

Read I Timothy 3:8-13. A godly gentleman in the congregation in which I grew up never would allow himself to be called to the position of deacon. He believed that since he had been unsuccessful training his children to be believers in the Lord Jesus, he was disqualified from this office. The congregation was ready to call and bless him for ministry, but he flatly refused. Are there ways you have resisted being called and blessed? Why?

Pray that your spirit will be ready and willing to serve God in this ministry.

SENT OUT WITH INSTRUCTIONS

Choosing Leaders in the New Testament

We remember the institution of the first deacons in Acts 6:1-6. However, we often don't remember how these deacons were chosen. According to Luke, the apostles invited the whole community of disciples together and explained why they needed help. Then they asked the community to select from among themselves "seven men of good standing, full of the Spirit and of wisdom, whom we may appoint to this task" (Acts 6:3). Then, to make these appointments official, the seven men who had been chosen stood "before the apostles, who prayed and laid their hands on them" in blessing (Acts 6:6).

Leadership Selection among the Early Anabaptists

In the *Dordrecht Confession* of 1632, the laying on of hands already was prescribed as the way leaders were to be formally recognized and blessed for their task. Later, in the eighteenth and nineteenth centuries in Canada, immigration and new settlements soon required new leaders. In Upper Canada members of a church were nominated to be deacons, ministers, or bishops. If there were more nominees than needed, the lot was used.

In referring to the affirmation of deacons in the congregation, the *Ordinal* (1987) says, "Today this group is generally not ordained or commissioned, though in some situations deacons have been ordained for life" (17). However, today deacons and elders still are chosen from within the congregation.

But what did (and does) the service look like for the affirmation of elders or deacons? Following the tradition described in the *Dordrecht Confession*, the *Minister's Manual* of 1983 incorporated a service for the installation of elders/deacons that included the laying on of hands. In the *Confession of Faith in a Mennonite Perspective*, Article 15 also suggests that laying on of hands and ordination, or a similar act, is to be conducted as a sign of the person's accountability to the congregation and conference, as well as blessing and support. This statement is quite unclear as to whether different modes of affirmation are appropriate for the different ministerial leadership offices in the church. Whereas the 1983 *Minister's Manual* included a service for installing deacons, the *Minister's Manual* of 1998 now has a service of commissioning.

Through the centuries, Anabaptists have called lay leaders from within the congregation and ordained them for lifelong ministry. However, in recent years this has changed dramatically. Beginning in the second half of the twentieth century, deacons began to have limited terms of service, often three years. At the same time, various methods for blessing these lay leaders appeared in ministers manuals. Some elders and deacons were installed; some were commissioned. Through all the changes, the laying on of hands has remained part of the congregation's blessing for this office. According to recent church statements, the office of elder/deacon seems secure in church polity. Those chosen likely will continue to serve terms and not be ordained for life as in past tradition.

Calling Elders and Deacons Today

We know the qualifications for elders/deacons listed by Paul in the pastoral epistles. First Timothy 3:8-13 says a deacon "must be serious." Deacons must have established integrity in the community. They also must be single-minded in the faith, not following false pursuits, and they must have good relationships with their own families, which translates into good relationships with others as well. Above all, an elder/deacon must be trustworthy or faithful in all things. Paul speaks eloquently to the moral and spiritual qualifications, but there is more to the calling than being upright. There is also a calling to ministry.

Of this call, Norman Shawchuck and Roger Heuser write in *Leading the Congregation*: "The call beckons. No matter how tough the situation, no matter what is done or said, no matter how intense the trial—one must obey. The call to leadership is a formation process through which God uses all of life's experiences to sharpen and expand our leadership abilities" (67). How does the congregation choose moral and spiritual persons who also have the gifts for ministry the congregation needs?

In addition to the questions already raised, we also need to ask a different set of questions regarding ministry, such as:

1. *Who is currently doing ministry in this congregation?* Think broadly. Who is the one person who seems to do a good job of connecting with those who are ill? Who reaches out to new persons when they come? Who has a spiritual word of encouragement for you? These are the persons currently ministering in your congrega-

tion. In calling them to be elders/deacons, we give them authority to go forward and do the same on behalf of the congregation.

2. *Who has an inner calling to provide ministry?* Perhaps we need to call elders and deacons as we do pastoral leaders. This would mean that elders/deacons should share the story of their call to ministry with the congregation, just as pastors do. It is important that each elder or deacon has both an inner calling from God and an outer calling from the congregation.

3. *Has the congregation clearly identified the kinds of ministry it values? Who can provide those particular ministries?* If the congregation has identified community outreach as a high priority, then who can do that? If the congregation values someone to relate specifically to young adults, then who is gifted in that? What is the ministry of this congregation? What gifts does the pastor bring to this ministry, and what other gifts are needed? If the leadership of the congregation—the pastor(s), elders, and deacons—are not gifted or energized to provide ministry in line with the mission of the church, then the congregational vision for ministry will go nowhere.

4. *Who is being tapped on the shoulder to be trained for church leadership as an elder/deacon?* Lay leaders need to be representative of the people within the congregation. It is not true to biblical teaching or to Anabaptist tradition that a person must be at least forty years old to be an elder or deacon. All the groupings in the congregation need to see leadership that represents them.

What Do You Do When Finding Willing Leaders Is Difficult?

There are times in congregational life when it is difficult to call qualified persons to serve as elders or deacons. At these times self-examination is in order to detect possible causes for persons turning away from this essential ministry. Things to look for might include:

1. *The task is too large.* Too often we ask a few persons to shoulder a heavy responsibility. More minds, hearts, and shoulders make ministry more fulfilling. Perhaps the congregation needs more deacons or elders so each one can do one piece. First Mennonite Church in Winnipeg, Manitoba, has twenty deacons in

order to provide sufficient ministry to the 1,280 persons for whom they are responsible.

2. *The task is not specific enough.* Few congregations have taken the time to develop a sufficiently detailed job description so that persons being called to consider the office of elder/deacon know what is being asked of them. Good candidates may be wary to commit to what is unknown. A job description not only gives energy to the ministry of the elder/deacon board, but also provides boundaries that help define and confine responsibilities.

3. *The task is not challenging.* If the board appears to simply rubber-stamp decisions, which allows the pastor to be the only person involved in significant ministry, then good candidates will not be challenged and will find other avenues for ministry. The elder/deacon role is large. Look back at the ministry responsibilities listed in the Bible and assumed in Anabaptist congregational life (see session 2) to be reminded of what elders and deacons have been called to do.

4. *The congregation is not thinking broadly enough about who can minister.* What are the hidden understandings of the congregation about who is suitable to be called for this office? Is the list of qualifications too narrow?

5. *The congregation is not growing leaders nor calling persons to ministry.* Every congregation must continue to call leaders from within. There is no store or factory somewhere manufacturing pastors or elders or deacons. So if developing leadership is a congregational responsibility, how is that happening in your setting? Who is taking responsibility in your congregation to ensure that this happens? When this calling is taken seriously, people are invited to consider elder/deacon positions and perhaps pastoral positions as well.

6. *The history of conflict makes all sensible persons run the other way.* When previous boards have spent the bulk of their meeting time and most of their emotional energy managing conflict within the congregation, few persons get excited about being called to be an elder or deacon. If this is the situation, then a new strategy for managing conflict is a must, using an outside resource. ⸙

7. *Time constraints.* Few elders or deacons have unlimited time to give to the church. Therefore, to maintain the amount of time needed for this ministry the number of meetings must be limited. Additionally, meeting time often gets gorged with administrative details so little time is left for spiritual development or ministry. Reorganize meetings. For example, if you meet twice each month, schedule one meeting for support of the pastor and oversight of the congregation. Then keep the second meeting for ministry and spiritual growth. Always maintain balance between ministry and administration.

As You Go

1. What are three different ways elders/deacons can be chosen by a congregation? Think broadly.

2. How are elders/deacons chosen in your congregation? Does this method work well? What are its strengths and its drawbacks? If necessary, how could this current method be changed?

3. Do you feel that the commissioning or installation service conducted in your congregation gave you the authority you need to do your work effectively?

4. What is the age range of your elder/deacon group? What are the reasons individuals in your group were chosen?

Working Together as a Ministry Team

THESE TWELVE JESUS SENT OUT

Spelling out the expectations for members of a church board can be a laborious task. But until we clarify what we require or expect, we are certain to disappoint one another, as well as the people we serve. The prophet Micah knew that God has expectations. Read Micah 6:8. Since God requires certain things of us, it is reasonable for us also to require certain understandings and behaviors of our colleagues.

Pray that each one on the team will be honest and open in discussing common commitments for the Elder/Deacon Covenant. And pray that you will not be defensive but will be an example of openness in your negotiations.

SENT OUT WITH INSTRUCTIONS

Defining the Working Relationship

God provided a covenant so Israel would know what to expect from God and so God could describe what was expected from Israel. The covenant was meant to define their working relationship. Likewise, deacons and elders need to specify their understanding of what it means to work together as leaders of a congregation. Few leadership groups argue over what needs to be done; but many disagree over how ministry should be done. Therefore, the purpose of a deacon/elder covenant is to bring to the fore hidden assumptions about how to provide the ministry the deacons/elders have been called to give to the congregation.

Writing a covenant also is a means by which a deacon/elder group may get to know one another. An instrument such as this makes it possible to include gifted persons who may not share the same historical, ethnic, or religious background but have been rightly called to the office of elder or deacon. The goal of having a covenant is to build trust and make it possible for the team as a whole to experience success in their ministry. Writing the covenant likely will take more than one hour, so allow adequate time. Remember, this covenant must be revised and adopted by the entire group annually, incorporating the counsel of each new leader who begins a term. It is unfair to assume that new elders or deacons automatically give assent to what has been written before.

Once the covenant has been agreed upon and signed by each elder or deacon, each one should receive a copy. It may be presented to the congregation for their information, but it is not a covenant between the elders and the congregation, since the congregation was not part of the conversation that formulated the agreement. However, keep in mind that the covenant must incorporate broad congregational expectations of the deacon/elder team. The covenant includes the pastor(s), but in a congregation with a pastoral team all pastors may have an additional covenant that applies specifically to their own responsibilities.

As You Go

Leadership Team Covenant

Each section below contains questions to help you write your covenant. Some sections have a commentary to help you reflect.

Answer the questions before you read the commentary so you will be aware of the natural tendencies of your group. An abbreviated covenant form without the commentary can be found in Appendix B.

Regarding the true essence of the covenant, James W. Fowler writes in *Faith Development and Pastoral Care*: "In a covenant community [such as deacons/elders/pastors] persons with different callings are bound together with common loyalties to a cause or to beliefs and values that are bigger than they. It does not particularly matter whether the persons like one another or not. It is not important whether they would have chosen to be yoked together or tied up with these particular others or not. In a covenant community, for the sake of the shared loyalty to the cause for which the community came into being, they work at relations of mutual trust with their companions in community, and with the cause that animates its purpose" (35).

1. Spiritual Commitments to Each Other
- How will the deacons/elders care for each other's spiritual life?
- How will you be accountable to each other for a healthy spiritual life?
- What do you commit to do for your own spiritual growth?

2. Deacon/Elder Meetings
- What are the expectations of the group for attendance?
- What is an acceptable reason for missing?
- How often will the team meet?
- How long will each meeting last?
- Who will chair the meetings?
- Who will prepare the agenda?
- How does a member of the team get an item placed on the agenda?

3. Public Decorum
- How will the team act or speak in public or with individuals

if they together or individually cannot agree with an action taken by the congregation or the pastor(s)?

4. Confidentiality

- Information is power. How will that power be shared?
- How far is information shared on the team?
- Will permission of persons involved always be sought before information is shared? Is there any circumstance in which information may be shared without permission?
- Are deacons and elders free to share information with spouses or significant others? Does the pastor share confidential information with the deacons and elders?
- Are these guidelines made known up front to individuals and the congregation?

Confidentiality is one of the nebulous battlegrounds in team ministry, for it is replete with landmines. Therefore, before a hot situation arises, decide how far your circle of confidentiality will extend.

If the team decides that each one will maintain alone what he or she is told in the course of pastoral care work, then the entire leadership group needs to agree to it. The congregation should be made aware of the understanding so a congregational member won't talk to another deacon or elder as if they too know the whole story. If confidences that seem too heavy to carry alone are shared just within the team, then that too should be understood. Trust with the congregation must never be violated.

The key to keeping confidence is recognizing that what you know is power. If the deacons and elders recognize they are dealing with a personal power issue, then they can work to limit their own personal power agenda and not hurt others in the process.

A person's story really belongs to that person alone, and he or she should be able to delineate who hears the story and who is not privy to it. *A Mennonite Polity for Ministerial Leadership* warns that "confidentiality requires vigilance. Disciplinary action may be brought against a minister for violations of confidentiality. Pastors and deacons/elders develop understandings with each other around what is appropriately shared in a deacon/elder's meeting. When dealing with members who are ill or in the hospital, the pastor does not pass on patient information without permission from the patient; if the patient is unable to speak for him/herself, the family gives such permission" (112).

5. Conflict
- How will disagreements be handled?
- What outside person/resource will be used to help process conflict?

It is inevitable that a group of persons, even deacons and elders, will not always agree. Therefore, before this happens, decide how internal group disagreements will be addressed by formulating a process.

For example, agree to use the Matthew 18 process of going first to the person with whom you have a conflict. Then, if the person will not hear you, invite another elder or deacon to sit in on your discussion as you try to hear everyone's position. Finally, if agreement still is not reached, invite the entire leadership group to hear both parties' concerns and to help the two involved understand each other. If conflict involves the entire group or if the board is sharply divided, utilize an outside resource person, such as a conference minister or trained mediator. *A Mennonite Polity for Ministerial Leadership* says, "During congregational conflict, the pastor, deacons/elders and conference minister seek outside assistance, preferable someone skilled in conflict management/resolution/mediation" (117). It is extremely important to set this up *before* conflict occurs.

An example of a covenant agreement may look like this: "We covenant to work out our problems as a deacon/elder team, take the initiative to settle our disputes among ourselves, and seek help from _____ when needed to resolve our differences, in order to represent our ministry to the congregation as the work of a united team."

6. Complaints

- How will an individual deacon/elder receive complaints from congregational members?
- How will an individual deacon/elder receive complaints about other deacons or elders?
- To whom or where should complaints be directed?
- Will the deacon/elder group hear and respond to anonymous complaints?
- How will anonymous letters and complaints be handled?

Believe it or not, the leadership group is not called to be a complaint office. If the fundamental responsibility of the deacon board is to fix problems as they arise in the congregation, then be assured that is all the board will get done. You will spend all your time answering these questions: Who wants what? How do we satisfy this group or person? What should we do about this problem or complaint?

The goal is to minimize problem questions and refocus on purpose and identity questions. These questions need not be answered as part of this covenant, but are also an important contributor to the working cohesion of the deacon/elder group:

- Who are we, and what are we called to be?
- What are we called to do in this chapter of our history as a congregation?
- What are the goals and objectives we set out to accomplish in our ministry?
- What are the appropriate strategies for our ministry?

If all you do is solve problems, then you will be given problems and complaints to solve. This can be an extremely discouraging treadmill. Instead, learn to make decisions based on your understanding of the congregation's call to ministry rather than to an individual's or group's preferences. This often means managing differences in the congregation rather than harmonizing them, or managing differences in order to preserve them rather than negotiating differences into common agreement

Deacons and elders also need to be aware of carrying complaints for others. A Mennonite Polity for Ministerial Leadership is helpful in this area. It says: "All church leaders have a responsibility to model and coach others to speak the truth in love, avoiding the tendency to 'triangle' others into one's concerns (telling a third party what one should rightly tell the person [or group] who offended you). Deacons/elders encourage members to speak directly with the minister about concerns related to the minister, rather than speaking indirectly to the minister through the deacons/elders. In almost all cases, Jesus' instructions about going first to the brother or sister who has offended you (Matt. 18:15-20) are the basis for such truth telling. And the truth telling involves showing the person your identity when you go to them. Therefore, anonymous letters or complaints do not fit into the Matthew 18 teaching since the identity of the complainant must be known. A leader does not repeat the complaint to others on behalf of the person offended, but rather helps the person offended speak the truth for him/herself" (112).

7. Accountability

Deacon/elder team members are first accountable to each other for making the team ministry a success. All members are equal in this accountability, even the team leader.

- Will you agree to be accountable to each other for your words, your actions, and your spiritual life?

8. Collaborative Ways of Thinking

When a group endeavors to work together, every action must be weighed by how it will affect the others. Therefore, a good team of deacons or elders is interested in finding out what other members think on almost every question. In so doing the group develops a corporate way of thinking. This means that the leadership group needs to discern congregational direction together, plan ways of implementing the direction together, and expect each one's direct involvement in getting the work done. Discerning together, planning together, and passing it on to the pastor to get it done is appropriate some of the time, but not all of the time. If individuals don't think corporately, things will be done singularly and alone. Collaborative thinking leads to group decisions and takes group responsibility for those decisions and actions. Collaborative thinking also requires that everyone talk together. It takes only one person who will not talk during the discussion or who only talks after the meetings for the collective strength to be diminished. Collaboration requires sharing power and being accountable for that power. In the same way, actions or promises made by one deacon or elder on behalf of the group are accountable to the group and must be named. When we think collaboratively we work and are sustained as parts of a whole.

- What agreements can you make about how everyone will participate in group decisions, discussion, and ministry?
- Are there any times when an individual deacon or elder may speak on behalf of the entire group without first speaking to the group?

9. Sexuality

As the church develops new ministries and leadership structures, it has become inevitable that women and men often end up working together. Deacon/elder groups also have experienced this change. Modeling healthy male/female relationships is part of the holy calling to serve as a leader in the church. It is wise for deacons and elders to make an agreement together to cover working relationships both within the deacon/elder group and with those with whom we minister. There is an extremely fine line in ministry between helping someone and boosting our own ego. It is flattering to our ego to know someone needs us and that we can help. So we have to constantly monitor our actions, thought patterns, and feelings to be honest about our motivation for ministry. Put inappropriate sexual expression out on the table and talk about it. This kind of discussion not only encourages accountability but also clears the air among our own interactions.

- Agree that inappropriate sexual expression has no place in our ministering relationships.
- Agree to be honest when you see one of you spending too much time with a member of the congregation.

- Agree to be candid when another deacon or elder tells a joke or makes a comment or gesture that makes you uncomfortable.
- What are the physical actions, words, jokes, or personal information that you consider appropriate or inappropriate to share? In the deacon/elder circle? In the congregation? How does sexual inappropriateness affect your ministry, especially in home visitation?

If you make this agreement up front, then you shouldn't have to second guess another person's motives or look for innuendo in what he or she says or does. However, this will take some continued talking. For example, some persons are comfortable giving hugs. But for others a hug can feel like a sexual expression they would prefer to avoid. So it is important not only to set ground rules, but also to be honest and delineate what that means for your working relationship. The church demands that we work together in the most holy way, and that includes our sexuality.

10. Congregational Commitments
- In summary, in light of these agreements, what does the deacon/elder team commit to the congregation (i.e., regular prayer, modeling healthy relationships, availability, etc.)?

Ministry Skills:

Spiritual Oversight for Decision Making

THESE TWELVE JESUS SENT OUT

Over and over again in the early church, decisions regarding a course of action or appointments of persons to positions of leadership were made with prayer and fasting. Read Acts 14:21-23 and 20:17-38. In both situations elders/deacons were part of the inner circle making decisions with church leadership, and they were part of a prayer circle. When making decisions in your own life, what do you pray for?

Pray that decisions that need to be made in the near future in your congregation will be more than just debates and will be accompanied by time to listen to God.

SENT OUT WITH INSTRUCTIONS

A Uniquely Spiritual Calling

Spiritual oversight has become a nonspecific term with little concrete interpretation in congregational leadership. As a result it often has been interpreted in a functional manner to include administrative oversight of the congregation's committees or com-missions. This trend has left elder/deacon teams exhausted and unsure of how their role is significantly different from that of the church council. Consequently, many elders and deacons have lost the uniquely spiritual aspect of their calling and focus.

The two areas the elder/deacon team must take primary respon-sibility for are the spiritual dimension of congregational decision making and the development and maintenance of congregational vision. If this leadership group does not provide oversight for these two crucial areas of congregational life, then no one will; no other group usually is given specific mandate for the body life.

Spiritual Oversight in Decision Making among Leaders

Providing spiritual oversight begins with good decision making on the elder/deacon board. If this group is not tuned in to God's leading, it will be impossible to lead a congregation in a Holy Spirit-directed decision-making process. This means that prayer is the first step. The truth is that congregations only will take time to pray to the extent that the congregational leadership group prays for the persons in their care, the church community as a whole, and about the decisions they make on a regular basis.

- Does your board of elders or deacons have a spiritual life?
- Are you conversant with one anothers' spiritual lives?
- Do you share spiritual experiences on a regular basis to rein-force that God is a sought-after contributor to your life and your group?

Here are several suggestions for how you can do that:

1. *Practice awareness of God's presence.* At the beginning of the meeting, offer opportunity for all elders/deacons to identify an occasion since the last meeting when they were aware of God's presence or activity in their own lives, in the church, or in the community.

2. *Tell faith stories.* Request that each elder or deacon share his or her faith story, perhaps one each month. Too often we don't know much about the spiritual life of others, and we don't have a systematic way of asking.

3. *Write the spiritual story of the congregation.* We easily can write the story of the church building and its repairs over the past ten years. Perhaps more important would be to write the spiritual story of the congregation over the past ten years.

4. *Pray about decisions.* Leaders need to make frequent decisions, but too often they are made hurriedly and without much time spent in prayer. Be committed to praying for decisions, as well as for pastoral care concerns.

5. *Structure meetings.* One method of controlling the speed of decision making is to structure meetings so that prayer and decision making are given separate space and time. For example, agree to make decisions in two steps. In the first meeting build the agenda outlining the decisions that need to be made, pray about each item, and pray for each other. Then wait for the next meeting to make the decisions. This approach can be much more efficient as well.

Good leadership is a spiritual task. That is why leading the congregation requires continually being led by the Holy Spirit. Since leadership is not a science, effective congregational leadership relies not so much on exact methods and formulas as it does on judgment, common sense, values, and intuition—all informed by the Holy Spirit. That is why discernment can be understood only in spiritual terms, using such spiritual methods as faith stories and prayer.

Spiritual Oversight in Congregational Decision Making

Elders and deacons have much more influence in the congregation than they generally assume, especially in the area of spiritual practice. Therefore, it is the spiritual responsibility of the elder/deacon team to advocate for prayer before any discernment process in the congregation. Why pray before congregational decision making?

1. *Prayer puts the decision into words.* It helps prepare our minds to think through the decisions that need to be made. If we have taken time to talk with God about the decision, we will have verbalized the question at least to ourselves in prayer, thereby indi-

cating whether we understand it or not. Often we are not sure exactly what the problem is until we try to explain it. That is when we learn how complicated it is and how difficult it is to explain it easily, even to God, who understands all. Prayer forces us to put the question into our own words.

2. *The answer belongs to God.* By deliberately going to God in prayer, we are acknowledging that God has an answer to this question. We may not have an answer at this time, but we recognize God's hands contain all of life.

3. *Prayer requires us to give up our own ideas.* Going to God for guidance helps us let go of our notion of what the outcome of the decision should be. It is impossible to authentically meet God and tell God what needs to be done. If we find we are doing this in our prayer life, then we have assumed the place of God.

4. *Prayer connects us to the love of God.* It is only in the context of God's love that we discover the power to embrace the other and yet allow the other to remain the other. We don't have to change everyone else's mind to think as we do. Instead, we need to find out the mind of God, and the Holy Spirit will help us.

5. *Prayer reaffirms the vision and mission of our congregation.* Each time we meet we need to be reminded of who we are, what we are about in this congregation and this world, and what we are and are not responsible for. Reaffirming the vision reminds us of our boundaries. Prayer helps us accomplish that task as well.

Working through Congregational Resistance

Interestingly enough, while we all admit to needing prayer and God's guidance, there often remains incredible resistance to praying for any length of time in the congregation. This is especially true if prayer seems to be only an exercise and if it lengthens the meeting time considerably. Why might the congregation resist prayer?

1. *People are not comfortable praying.*

2. *People come with fears regarding decisions.* It may be helpful to lead the congregation to identify its fears and name them. This is especially important with issues that are highly charged.

Allow persons to express their fears in small groups first.

3. *Prayer could lead to inaction if people do not feel led by the Spirit.*

4. *Prayer has been ineffective in the past since people still took sides in the conflict.* Spiritual oversight requires that elders and deacons not allow prayer to be simply a time out before everyone goes back to their respective corner for the fight. It must be understood in the congregational decision-making process that persons come ready to empty themselves and hear the word of God and the community.

5. *Prayer is too boring.* Prayer must be serious but not solemn. Laughter in prayer and decision making indicates we recognize that God is ultimately in control and that we must not hold our positions so tightly that we don't give God space to work.

Suggestions for Organizing Prayer Time

1. *Outline the agenda several weeks before the meeting and ask for specific volunteers to commit themselves to pray for each item.*

2. *List at the beginning of the meeting the crucial decisions that need to be made.* Determine where prayer groups for each item will meet, and invite each person to go to the prayer group for the decision that most concerns her or him. In this way congregational members will be able to pray about what raises the most fear within them. Secondarily, it is a good way for leadership to monitor which issues have raised the most concern. If more people pray for the student aid fund than for the building project, then you know which issue will heighten emotions.

3. *Announce that the meeting will begin with fifteen minutes of silent prayer to allow the Holy Spirit to work.*

4. *Designate a person to lead in prayer at the beginning of the discussion and follow with a few moments of silent prayer.* Do this for each item on the agenda.

Prayers or conversations with God are not a mere formality so we can get church meetings going. Conversing with God affects every area of our life together as God's people. It is one area to which we have not been as attentive as we should.

As You Go

1. What kind of decision-making process does the leadership group presently use? Write down the steps currently used when the leadership team makes a decision.

2. How much time do elders/deacons now put into prayer for decisions they are required to make? There are few leadership groups around anymore that haven't agonized over church discipline. Do you spend as much time in prayer as you do in discussion?

3. How would you change the process you now use? What other methods could be considered? What are the advantages and disadvantages of these other methods compared to the one currently being used?

4. Trace an important decision your congregation made recently. Reflect on the key players in making this decision. Who were they? What were their feelings? What roles were they playing?

Ministry Skills:

Vision for Ministry

THESE TWELVE JESUS SENT OUT

The prophet Joel promised that because of the pouring out of God's Spirit all of God's people will prophesy, dream dreams, and see visions. Read Joel 2:27-29. What is the dream or vision the Holy Spirit has given to you? Are you acting on this vision?

Pray that the ministry team with which you serve will be filled with God's Spirit so you will know unity of vision and move on it.

SENT OUT WITH INSTRUCTIONS

Creators and Keepers of the Vision

Spiritual oversight includes not only proactive leadership of the congregation during times of decision making, but oversight is also crucial when formulating vision for ministry and mission. If the deacon/elder team of the church does not take leadership for creating and sustaining vision, then who will? This perhaps may be the most crucial task of the team. If a congregation does not have a vision for its mission, it will flounder and too often tear itself apart through conflict. If you don't want the congregation to be inwardly focused, then the deacon/elder team must give the people vision to embrace an outward mission. A definition of *spiritual oversight* from Pastorate Project includes "discerning the spiritual needs in the body and helping the congregation to develop and keep in focus its vision for its gathered life and its scattered life and total mission" (20).

Various writers have tried to arrive at distinct definitions for *mission, vision,* and *ministry,* often resulting in more confusion than clarity. In this session we will assume that these three words are quite close in meaning, and so will use them interchangeably.

Who Leads the Visioning Process?

Dreaming comes naturally to some persons, but it is not a common characteristic of institutions. In fact, institutions such as the church spend most of their energy trying to maintain current programs, not reaching out to new missions. This is where the image of the body works so well and illustrates the dilemma we face. The church is an institution, but at the same time it is a living, changing organism. There always will be people in the church with compassion, who in spite of all odds do incredible ministry in such places as jails, hospices, and refugee resettlement projects. So we have the static institution on one hand and the living organism on the other. This means we cannot expect the static institution to project a need for vision. That is not its personality. But we can tap into the living organism of the body for this to happen.

As leaders we cannot wait for the church council to put vision-making on its agenda—in all likelihood that will never happen. The process of creating vision is totally dependent on congregational leadership, and the success of creating vision is dependent on congregational involvement. It is the function of leadership to *affect* the congregation so that their resources are energized and their functions are promoted. Because of leadership's role in the congregation, it is usually only those in leadership who can most effect calmness, focus, and change. So the question for leadership is: What can you do to make the congregation dream a dream? If dreaming isn't happening, we must ask why not. What are you not doing to create time, space, and energy for that to happen?

Congregational size and cultural dynamics also affect the course of creating vision. Small churches tend to have more vested in a congregationally-determined vision, even though the deacon/elder/ pastor team still needs to lead the process. The larger the congregation, the more likely those in leadership will determine the vision. Regardless of these dynamics, the bottom line is that leadership must lead in the process of determining the congregation's vision. Once a vision is in place, the leadership team serves as stewards of the vision. By continually articulating a sense of where the congregation is going, the leadership group keeps the direction and goals in the congregation's field of vision. The leadership team is responsible to continue to ask crucial questions about how vision is affecting congregational decisions and mission.

What Is Vision?

Vision identifies both identity and direction for mission.

Vision establishes identity through seeing what exists now in your congregation. Identity is established through claiming the strengths and unique gifts of your particular congregation. What do you do well? What is important to the congregation that you do well? Vision is the ability to see what is.

By knowing what is, we can develop plans for where we are going. Vision also gives us direction, a map for where we are going. Churches with a strong sense of identity and a clear purpose fueled by energy are the ones that are inviting and growing. Identity and direction are the keynotes to vision and health.

Qualities of a Good Vision Statement

1. *A good vision statement clarifies the identity of a congregation and its core processes* while allowing congregational leaders to ask how each effort or program will either reach out and receive people, relate them to God, nurture them in discipleship, or send them out prepared for service. Consider this vision statement of the prophet Habakkuk:

Then the Lord answered me and said:
Write the vision; make it plain on tablets,
  so that a runner may read it.
For there is still a vision for the appointed time;
  it speaks of the end, and does not lie.
      (Habakkuk 2:2-3a)

God is the reference point for this vision. It is not simply Habakkuk's dream for the future, but God's answer to his questions about the future.

2. *The vision has to originate from a group or person whose identity is known and clear.* This particular vision comes from God. God obviously knows who God is, and the people do too. The writer says of God: "Are you not from of old, O Lord my God, my Holy One? You shall not die" (Habakkuk 1:12a).

3. *The vision needs to be written down.* It is not enough anymore to assume that everyone in the church automatically knows what the church is about. With increased diversity in our congregations, diverse ideas emerge about what the church is supposed to be doing. We are setting ourselves up for conflict when we operate with numerous unspoken assumptions. In Habakkuk's time the vision was written on clay tablets and then baked or dried so the writing would be made permanent.

4. *The vision has to be easily understood.* This should not be a complicated statement designed for congregational theologians. The vision needs to be understood on the run, and needs to be simple enough to carry it along, as it was in Habakkuk's setting.

5. *The mission needs to be time specific.* There is a temptation to make mission statements so nebulous that they do not provide enough structure and guidance for a specific time. God encouraged Habakkuk with a vision for an appointed time.

6. *Mission statements need to be future-oriented.* God told Habakkuk that the vision spoke of the end, of a time when the Chaldeans, who were bringing violence and destruction upon the land, would be stopped.

7. *A vision statement must have integrity.* It cannot be a frivo-

lous congregational exercise, but rather a sincere discerning of God's will for the future.

8. *If the vision is meant to be a congregational vision, it must be accepted, adopted, and celebrated by the whole congregation, not just by those who led the process.* It was easy for Habakkuk to embrace this vision and act on it; the vision came to fruition shortly after Habakkuk's time with the fall of the Southern Kingdom. The principle holds true in the congregation as well.

As You Go

A Process for Visioning

Preparation Phase

Begin with prayer. Vision comes from God. Unless we commit ourselves to seek God's face earnestly, we will have a vision that is only of our own making. Prayer will not only be needed at the beginning of the process but all the way through. The process needs to be outlined clearly and simply so it can not only be understood and accepted, but embraced by the congregation. This includes a time frame, as well as proposed steps of action.

Embarking on a visioning process needs to be a congregational decision because the unauthorized dreaming of only a few will cause endless conflict. This isn't meant to be a contest of dueling dreams with winners and losers. This is more akin to a plan of action agreed upon by a group of people.

Research Phase 1: Identity for Mission

For dreams to have integrity, they must be based in the reality of where you have come from, who you are now, and what your potential is in this world and in God's sight. Earlier generations had assumptions about what congregations were. Those assumptions worked for hundreds of years, helping Christian men and women carry out what they understood mission to be in their time. Those assumptions led to the establishment of institutions and structures in addition to congregations, all shaped by the church's concern to build Christendom. In our times many of these assumptions no longer work, which leads to increased trouble in our congregations and the institutions around them.

This question pushes us to look at the roots of why we need congregations.

Biblical Identity of the Church

What is our mandate as the church? Sometimes this is found in the membership covenant of a congregation. But it can't rest there. In almost every example of the New Testament church, Jesus helped define identity for his followers. For example, Jesus told his followers in the Sermon on the Mount: "You are the salt of the earth" and "You are the light of the world" (Matthew 5:13-14). Both statements speak to biblical identity as God's people.

For a congregation to have a clear biblical identity, it requires good teaching and good preaching to present and reaffirm the gospel, the biblical story. This is the responsibility of congregational leadership, pastor and elders. This biblical identity is our bedrock upon which we can build a vision. A biblically illiterate congregation cannot create a vision with integrity.

Local Identity

Not only do we need to know who we are as a people of God, but a congregation also is composed of identifiable individuals. So research to uncover the local identity of the congregation is also part of this process. You will want to know:
- How many persons are retired in your congregation?
- How many have young children?
- What is the level of education?
- How many are involved in service-oriented careers already?

The answers to all these questions make a difference in the kind of vision statement that will be composed. It is the answers to these questions that give ideas about future ministry to young adults, retired folks, or single parents, for example. It also lets us know who the congregation relates to on a daily basis in their work world. This is valuable information because it defines where the natural connections for evangelism occur.

Congregational Identity

Congregations also have a personality that informs their identity and affects their vision and how it is implemented.

- What personality traits best describe your congregation?
- How does your congregation handle conflict? Do they face it or flee?
- Does your congregation welcome entrepreneurial persons to begin new ministries?
- Do they like the spontaneous or the well-thought-out?

James Christopher has done extensive work on introverted and extroverted organizations. How do these characteristics apply to your congregation?

1. *Extroverted Churches*
   - Have more open boundaries and mixing of people and programs.
   - Can act quickly and think things out in the open on the go.
   - Take the spoken word as reliable communication.
   - Look outside for help when in trouble.
   - Express faith easily in public.

2. *Introverted Churches*
   - Have a clear sense of space, territory, and boundaries.
   - Like to reflect inwardly and test thinking with their group before acting.
   - Prefer written communication and documentation.
   - Draw a tight circle and look inside for help when in trouble.
   - Express faith more readily in a one-on-one, personal context.

You can see that the collective identity and personality of the congregation also has implications for creating a vision statement. Finding out who you are is hard but necessary work for the congregation.

Research Phase 2: Direction for Mission

Now that you have answered such identity questions as where you have come from as a biblical people and who you are today, you can begin to focus on the direction question. What is God calling you to do to build the kingdom in your locale? The vision has to be based on a real situation facing the congregation and the community.

Ask the congregation to brainstorm a list of needs they see in the congregation and the community. At this point there will be no comment or evaluation made of any suggestions.

Rewrite the lists so that common needs are grouped together.

Give each person three stickers to place beside the three needs with which they most identify.

Writing Phase

Invite leaders of every group in the congregation to submit in writing what they believe should be part of the vision statement for your congregation. It does not need to be a clear, complete statement, but a written description of the elements they feel would be essential to the vision statement. Encourage them to complete this task in light of their current congregational responsibility and to feel free to discuss it with other members of their committee.

Then invite a writer to compile the results. This is one church document that needs to be well-written. Hold a meeting for the congregation to respond to the proposed statements. The congregation needs to approve the final document.

Implementation Phase

Develop strategies. How can the vision statement meet a current need? This question must be placed before each committee in the church. For ownership to occur, each group should choose a phrase out of the vision statement that will be their priority for the coming year. From that priority each group will design strategies to reach that vision. Remember, vision has to do with the endpoint of where we want to go. Strategies and priorities have to do with how we are going to get there or the means to achieve those ends. Part of being in leadership is turning the vision into reality. Unfortunately, this is where vision usually gets lost!

Publish each committee's proposed plans resulting from the vision statement. You may want to display the annual goals or keep a record of them in a book each year. This is a good record of congregational mission and helpful for yearly evaluation.

Annual Review

The leadership team should lead an annual review of the vision statement.

First, *celebrate the successes of the year.* Have each person in the church make a list of things they want to celebrate. Compile a complete list of these suggestions.

Then, *acknowledge the failures.* Also allow committees to express their disappointment in ministries they planned that didn't materialize. Offer a prayer of confession and forgiveness.

Review how church structures are helping or hindering the successful attainment of your strategies.

There is no perfect vision and no perfect leader on this earth. From the biblical story we know that Abram clearly was not perfect, but he was a man with identity and direction. He had vision for the future of a nation, and the direction he walked to implement that vision was counted as righteousness. Hear a word of grace for pastors and church leaders: God is not judging you as harshly as you are judging yourselves. The question is: Is the direction you are going faithful to the God who calls you and to the congregation God has called you to be?

SESSION 7

Ministry Skills:

Mediating Conflict

THESE TWELVE JESUS SENT OUT

During your tenure as a deacon or elder, you may very well encounter a conflict such as the one between Paul and Barnabas. Read Acts 15:36-40. This disagreement was so sharp that the co-workers parted company. We have no hint that this was a mutual decision, but apparently it seemed to be the only answer. In your experience is this the best way to resolve a stalemate? How do you normally react to conflict when it is part of your own life?

In prayer listen to what God may be telling you about how you respond to conflict and what your role may be in your congregation regarding interpersonal tensions.

SENT OUT WITH INSTRUCTIONS

It Can Happen to Us

Conflict is certainly not a new experience among God's people. We all remember Cain and Abel. They fit well the definition of *interpersonal conflict* as "an expressed struggle between at least two interdependent parties who perceive incompatible goals, scarce resources and interference from others in achieving their goals" (*Interpersonal Conflict*, 41).

Conflict may have been the core of Cain and Abel's story, but we never really believe conflict will happen to our congregation or to us. That we assume it won't affect us is further evidence of our avoidance and fear of conflict. Most of us know how to run quickly from any sort of tension. We pretend we don't see the angry body language. We don't hear the stony silences. We refuse to speak about anything less than heaven in our personal and congregational relationships.

But as the people of God, we are called first to practice justice in relationships within the church itself. The early church tried to reconcile Jewish Christians and Gentile Christians. In a similar way the church today works to reconcile groups that are in conflict. It tries to bring them into right relationship with each other to achieve justice.

It is inevitable that elders and deacons, as congregational leaders, will be called upon to settle disputes. In former times when a congregation or individuals were fighting, the bishop or *Aeltester* would simply come and pronounce how the dilemma would be solved. Today we are constrained to hear all persons and lead them to a solution created and agreed upon together.

Although elders and deacons should not assume they can mediate serious conflict, each lay leader should have some knowledge of the mediation process and some rudimentary skill in leading it. If leaders have neither, they likely will not recognize conflict until it has escalated to a degree where resolution becomes difficult, and they will not understand the steps involved when a mediator comes in to help. When a third-party mediator is called in, it is the elders' and deacons' understanding of the mediation process that allows them to advocate for the process with those in the congregation who may be reluctant to become involved.

Stifling problems only gives them time to gain strength and fury. Allowing conflicts a safe place to be brought to light and discussed as early as possible increases the probability for resolution. But we have to know how and when to do that. Although people dislike conflict, differences of opinion are good and healthy because they allow greater understanding of ourselves and our world.

Interpersonal Conflicts and the Mediation Process

When dealt with early, conflicts often can be resolved before disagreements grow and gain supporters for each side. When individuals in the congregation are known to be in conflict, it is in the best interests of the congregation as a whole for leaders to take the initiative to address those involved. Rarely will persons come to the elders/deacons for assistance unless they are hoping to add support to "their" side. From there it is a short jump to being caught between two persons in conflict. Getting caught in the middle, or being "triangulated," involves carrying messages from one side to the other, being perceived as siding with both groups at the same time, and giving up the authority to call either side to accountable behavior. Taking the first step by going to those in conflict relieves the elder or deacon of being perceived as sympathetic to one side or the other and increases the possibility of resolving the conflict.

Effective resolution of conflict is dependent on the spiritual leader's ability to stay out of the issues and remain in the process. That is why being perceived as neutral is the key to success. Even when an outside mediator is called in, the elder/deacon only will be perceived as neutral if all the elders and deacons commit to following the process without criticism of the mediation facilitator.

When called to mediate, here are some basic steps to follow.

1. *Identify the people who will be involved in the mediation process.* Only these persons will be allowed to speak in this process. By limiting the persons involved, others are barred from entering through the back door to increase the clout of either side. Conflict can become complicated quite quickly when the primary players are not limited in number.

2. *Agree to ground rules.* Is everyone involved willing to follow the process? People ask for help in conflict not because they can envision a successful outcome or because they feel capable of being constructive, but because the pain has become unbearable.

That is why as soon as the pain of conflict has been slightly relieved, people will want to end the process. In general people are looking for a quick fix. This is one of the main reasons it is essential for everyone to agree at the beginning to follow the process and not opt out along the way. Persons involved must agree to not interrupt each other, be sarcastic, generalize about the situation (for example, insinuating that it happens all the time when that is likely not the case), accuse the other person, or call them names. Only the facilitator has permission to call attention to someone not adhering to the ground rules.

Persons involved should commit themselves to listening below the surface to realize their own needs, concerns, beliefs, and values, and the other person's as well. The listening skills outlined in session 8 should be used here as well. Furthermore, persons involved need to believe—completely—that the other person also is created in the image of God.

3. *Describe and summarize the conflict.* You might follow this pattern:

Person A: Describes how he/she experiences the conflict, using "I" statements.

Person B: Summarizes what Person A said.

Person B: Describes how she/he experiences the conflict, again using "I" statements.

Person A: Summarizes what Person B said.

4. *Describe and summarize resolution.* In this interchange the two parties talk about resolving the conflict:

Person A: Describes what resolution of this conflict would look like for him/her.

Person B: Summarizes what Person A said.

Person B: Describes what resolution would look like for her/him.

Person A: Summarizes what Person B said.

5. *Identify points of agreement.* What points of agreement exist for both persons? What next steps can be taken from these points of agreement?

6. *Write down future intentions for both persons.* Future inten-

tions include specific behaviors needed to maintain the agreement. For both parties to feel safe in the future, they each need to know what they can expect from the other person. Therefore, behavioral objectives should outline what each person will and will not do. This is also the place to decide what would be the appropriate action for each person if they perceive that the other person is not following through with the agreement.

7. *Schedule a follow-up session.* Set a time for the mediator to ask questions of both parties regarding the effectiveness of the resolution. Without such a time, accountability will go by the wayside, and old habits will be quick to return, and with them the conflict may come back.

Congregational Conflict

Healthy congregational leadership leads the way in using congregational resources and strengths to manage conflict. The leadership team cannot just sit quietly and hope it goes away.

Congregational conflict is often the result of individual conflict that has escalated to include the entire congregation. What may have started as one individual disagreeing with the pastor can quickly become two sides disagreeing over values. When this happens the scale of the conflict enlarges because the number of persons involved increases. At the same time, the point of disagreement can change from singing one particular song to a power struggle over who controls the music. This is also why it is in the best interests of the congregation to settle individual conflict before it grows.

Mediating congregational conflict is generally beyond the expertise of most elders or deacons. The dynamics and risks of mediating in a large group grow exponentially. Therefore, it is usually wisest for the congregation to contract with an outside mediator. Many congregational leaders balk at the cost of inviting in a professional mediator, but in doing so they rarely have counted the cost to the congregation of long-term conflict. During such times the congregation often loses its positive self-identity and replaces it with a negative one. For example, a congregation will begin to believe they are a bad group to join because members are always fighting. Pastors leave, and it is difficult to find a new pastor who wants to come into a conflict situation. Congregational members drift away to healthier congregations. Newcomers who step inside the front door of the church soon sense the conflict and do not return. Inviting a mediator to handle conflict early is often the best insurer of future congregational health.

In some conflicts over values, differences may not be reconcilable, and we may need to learn to live with our disagreements—we may need to learn how to agree to disagree (see Appendix C).

When to Call an Outside Mediator

Elder/deacon groups may want to be sure there is always someone in congregational leadership who has had mediation training. It will likely not work for this person to mediate congregational conflict, but that person could provide expert assistance in reading the level of conflict and in providing interpersonal mediation. Consider calling an outside mediator when:

- The elders and deacons as a team (or one of the team members) are not neutral and want to advocate a particular position.
- The issue is emotionally charged, and it will be difficult for one or the other conflicting parties to see that the leadership team is neutral.
- The conflict has escalated to the degree that the parties are polarized. This is a situation in which a third-party mediator absolutely must be called, because only someone who comes in as neutral can de-escalate such conflict.
- The conflict has changed from an individual conflict to a congregational conflict. At this point most of the congregation has become involved in the conflict.

As You Go

Most elders or deacons are reluctant to mediate interpersonal conflict not only because they are unsure of the mediation process, but also because they never have had an opportunity to do so. The safe confines of the leadership group is the perfect place to begin to experience the role of mediator.

In the following role-play scenario, choose one person to serve as mediator and one person to help participants remember the mediation process outlined above. Two other persons can play the parts of two congregational members in conflict (described below).

How would you mediate this conflict? Allow each elder or deacon to take a turn acting as the mediator.

How does your congregation respond financially to peacemaking? Susan Mark Landis suggests, "Review your congregation's commitment to peacemaking by analyzing the financial commitments of the congregation. What portion of the budget is devoted to peacemaking? Have you provided resources for peacemaking, both within and outside the congregation?"

Person A was elected to serve as Daily Vacation Bible School superintendent by the congregation. When looking for materials, Person A discovered that the Mennonite published materials were much more expensive than some other competitive publishers. Person A also was drawn to a study that included everyone in the congregation, children and adults alike, in reenacting the missionary journeys of Paul. It was even possible to do this study on a boat at a nearby lake, which would be a lot more fun than spending summer days in the church basement. Since Person A was in charge, he ordered the materials and started asking teachers.

Person B works in a city about forty miles from the church and was looking forward to dropping off her son and daughter at Daily Vacation Bible School, going to work, and then coming back to the church to pick them up later. When Person B found out that this year's Bible school was to be held at a nearby lake, she became quite panicked. She felt her children were safe at the church but not at a lake. After all, not every child knows how to swim, and who would be responsible to watch all those children near water? The additional discovery that the curriculum was not going to be Anabaptist, and that Anabaptist values might not be taught, was the last straw for Person B. Consequently, she is not allowing her children to go to Daily Vacation Bible School at all this year and is hoping to convince others in the congregation to follow suit.

Ministry Skills:

Visitation and Crisis Ministry

THESE TWELVE JESUS SENT OUT

Many will call out for your help. Many will assume you know what they need without them having to tell you. Jesus found both of these to be true in his ministry on this earth. Read Luke 18:35-43. Even though Jesus was the Son of God with divine powers of knowing, he still asked persons who came to him, "What do you want me to do for you?" (Luke 18:41). What do you want Jesus to do for you now?

Humility requires that we pray for God's wisdom as we visit and meet the needs of people in crisis, and that we ask those whom we serve the same question Jesus asked.

SENT OUT WITH INSTRUCTIONS

God's Visible Presence

In sharing ministry with the pastor(s) on the leadership team, deacons and elders often are called upon to visit congregational members who are in hospitals, care centers, or recuperating at home. They also may be asked to visit persons in the congregation who have recently welcomed children to their homes or suffered the loss of a family member. When deacons or elders visit in such a situation, their role is different than if they were visiting simply as a member of the congregation. They are providing an official ministry. Although this designation might be uncomfortable for the deacon/elder, it is essential to understand this role in order to fulfill this responsibility.

When visiting someone who is experiencing a crisis, you will need to be especially sensitive as to how long you should stay. Visiting for more than fifteen minutes in a hospital or thirty minutes in a home or care center may be a hardship for the one being visited. Again, ministry requires that deacons and elders meet someone else's needs and not their own.

In this time of visitation, you will want to hear the person's story, determine future ministry needs, offer to read Scripture, and pray.

With these specific tasks in mind, it is counterproductive to sit for endless hours with people unless they ask you to be there. Remember, the deacon/elder ministry is primarily a spiritual one. You are going to meet a spiritual need first, and all other needs are secondary. If you dilute your ministry with prolonged small talk and long hours poorly spent, then you have not accomplished what you went to do in the first place. You have been called to be God's visible presence for that person in the time of need, not simply a warm body filling time.

One more thing: If at all possible, call before you visit. Persons in crisis appreciate knowing you are coming so they prepare for your visit.

What Do I Say?

What frightens most people when anticipating visiting someone in crisis is the pressure to say the right thing. The good news is that the task of the deacon or elder is to listen in times of crisis, not to talk. This is not the time to be giving wise counsel or worn spiritual platitudes. Most often persons in crisis simply need to talk to someone who will really listen. In the case of a loss or a death, the only effective thing to say is, "I'm sorry." You can't fix the situation or act as if nothing has changed, but you can be sorry for what has occurred in the life of the person with whom you are sitting.

Listen to the Story

The object of visiting someone in crisis is to allow them to talk. This may make deacons or elders feel as if they are doing absolutely nothing for the person, which simply shows how much we undervalue listening. The task of the deacon or elder is to find out that person's story. Sometimes people are very open about sharing what is going on; other times, finding out their story can be a challenge.

Always remember that the person to whom you are listening must be the center of attention. Deacons or elders makes themselves the center of the conversation when they interrupt the speaker, tell their own stories, or give unsolicited opinions. Sometimes we do this in an attempt to show that we're listening or because of our own anxiety about the situation. In crisis situations, it is essential for the ministering person to be a calming presence; preparation and experience can help ensure that the focus remains on the other person.

Nonverbal communication can be a good way to indicate to the speaker that you are listening. You can convey this by maintaining eye contact with the speaker. You can indicate that you understand what the person is saying through nods and sincere facial expressions. Although you may not agree with the speaker, your ministry requires that you listen respectfully and with interest. Jesus provided a masterful example of this in his interaction with the Samaritan woman in John 4. Jesus asked simple questions and, without criticizing her, allowed the woman to tell what information she was comfortable revealing. Acceptance means giving support so the speaker is comfortable and able to continue to explore thoughts and share feelings.

Listening does not involve telling a comparable story. If you set up a story duel, you risk devaluing the story you have come to hear. Each story is unique and needs to be treated as such. If the one you are visiting has just had a gallbladder operation, you don't need to tell about your Aunt Tilly's horrendous experience and the size of her gallstones. When people are in crisis, their entire head and heart are working hard to assimilate their new experience. They do not have the energy nor the emotional and mental space to hear another's stories. For this reason, the deacon/elder must be disciplined enough to be a listener only.

In order to hear well, the deacon or elder may need to draw out the person's story with appropriate questions of clarification. This helps the listener to further understand the speaker's reaction to what is happening. It also gives the listener clues as to where the most tender spots may be. Such questions may be:

1. What do you mean by ...?
2. How did you feel afterward?
3. What did you think about that?
4. Would you do anything differently?
5. Tell me what happened.

Additionally, gentle questions may help the speaker focus his or her thoughts and feelings. It can help the person in crisis to say some things aloud that may have been kept inside until then. Perhaps now they can say, "I have no regrets about choosing this course of treatment." That alone can be powerful for the speaker to acknowledge. Often, telling the story aloud is one more step toward healing.

At the same time, listening does not include trying to change the person's perception about anything. What they tell you may be very different from the traffic accident report in the newspaper, but this is not the time to sort out the details. This is also not the time to ask about long-term plans. Questions about moving or finances are for later unless the person introduces the topic. Again, just listen—no matter how unrealistic the other person's current thinking may seem.

Persons under stress also can express beliefs about God that may seem heretical. They may say God doesn't care or God wouldn't allow such a devastating thing to happen. This is not the time to enter into a theological argument. You can offer to have faith for them when it is too difficult for them to have faith. But if deacons or elders try to correct the speaker's views on God, they will be dismissed as only interested in protecting religion and not as people who care for them.

Sometimes people accept that your questions are polite but may worry that you really are there only out of duty, that you want to know the details so you can go out and tell the neighborhood, or that you will be judgmental. As the listener it is your task to create a safe environment in which the person in crisis can talk without fear. The deacon or elder is meant to be the interested, caring receptacle of the speaker's story.

Accept and Respect Emotions

We can expend considerable effort trying to suppress or deny our emotions. However, for someone in crisis, words may be too much for the moment, and emotions may be all the person has. Giving people permission to feel their emotions and express them in your presence is a crucial form of listening.

It is especially important to allow people to mourn. We are in the wrong if another's mourning makes us feel uncomfortable and we try to derail this essential process. Jesus acknowledges the importance of mourning in Matthew 5:4 when he tells his disciples to bless those who mourn. He says nothing about trying to take people's minds off their grieving. We harm those who are mourning when we plan irrelevant activities solely to get someone's mind off her or his grief. Instead, we must learn how to participate in the mourning process so we will learn what it means to comfort others.

When people are disappointed or discouraged, don't tell them to cheer up. When people have suffered a significant loss, such as a death, don't tell them to look on the brighter side since their loved one is in heaven. Allow people to feel and acknowledge the sadness and grief they are experiencing.

Hear the emotions they are talking about and respond by validating their feelings. You can say, "You are telling me that you are angry." As a ministering person, such emotions may make you feel uncomfortable at times. But the emotions belong to the person you are visiting. If you do not allow people to experience their own hurt or anger, they will never be able to move on in the healing process. Paraphrase what they are telling you about their feelings and check to see if you have heard accurately. However, do not claim to understand what the person is going through. The truth is that none of us understands another person's pain. We all react to circumstances in different ways. To say we understand when we don't and can't trivializes the speaker's experience.

Use Touch Appropriately

Touch has become a difficult subject since physical abuse came to the forefront in church matters. However, there are persons who long for appropriate touch. This is especially true of people who reside in long-term care centers. Often one of the greatest losses for older persons is no longer having family members around who show their love through touch. In general, such persons appreciate you touching their arm or holding their hand when you pray.

In times of crisis sometimes a touch will mean more than any word that can be said. Ask the grieving person if you can give them a hug. Cover their hand with yours when you shake hands. However, some people do not like to be touched in any way by anybody. Be respectful of their choice. Also remember your agreements regarding touch in the Elder/Deacon Covenant. These should help you shape how you use touch in your ministry.

Read Scripture and Pray

Often persons who have been in crisis for a long time, such as in the middle of an extended hospital or care center stay, appreciate having Scripture read to them. Ask if it would be okay for you to read some Scripture. Have a passage chosen before you begin your visit; there is nothing worse than leafing through your Bible trying to find an appropriate passage while the person sits there and watches. This kind of behavior does not instill confidence in the ministry of the deacons/elders. Some appropriate Scripture passages for times of crisis include Psalms 103, 116, 121, 125, 130, and 139; and Isaiah 40 and 43.

Ask the persons you visit whether it would be acceptable for you to pray. If they agree, ask how you could best pray for them today. What is their greatest concern? Too many times deacons and elders shy away from this responsibility because of their own discomfort in praying aloud. However, the deacon/elder has been called to a spiritual ministry in the church that goes beyond friendship and providing meals to persons in troubled waters.

Determine Future Needs

In trying to determine continuing needs for the individual or family, go back to things that have arisen in your conversation. Offer the congregation's support and help. Persons in crisis generally find it easier to respond to a specific suggestion than such blanket statements as, "Call me if I can do anything for you." Come away with specific suggestions for help: a ride home from the hospital, childcare for a designated time, meals brought in, or assistance in contacting family members.

Promise the person you will get back to them when you have worked on the details. Make sure you follow through with your promise since you may be the only official link between the person and the congregation. It can be tempting to make false promises as an easy way to get out the door graciously. However, it is not gracious in the long run if you promise to return tomorrow and don't. So only make promises you are sure you can keep. Don't allow your integrity to break down as you are leaving. You need to keep it intact.

Confidentiality

People will trust deacons and elders with their stories if they know the deacons or elders have made a clear statement regarding confidentiality. This is the time to review and abide by your agreements in the Elder/Deacon Covenant. *A Mennonite Polity for Ministerial Leadership* advises, "When dealing with members who are ill or in the hospital, the pastor does not pass on patient information without permission from the patient; if the patient is unable to speak for him/herself, the family gives such permission" (112).

The bottom line is that the story belongs to the person in crisis and is their story to tell. It does not belong to pastors, elders, or deacons.

As You Go

Role-playing is the most helpful way to practice visiting a person in crisis. In pairs role-play how you would visit the persons described below. One person would be the deacon/elder and the other the person in crisis. Then trade roles and do it again. After both have had the opportunity to play each role, discuss these questions:

• What did you learn through this role-playing exercise?

• What was the most difficult part of your visit?

• Did you read Scripture and pray? Why or why not?

Scenario A

A woman with cancer is receiving chemotherapy and is quite proud of the way she is handling the situation. However, she gets angry at a friend in the church who constantly reminds her of other women who also seemed to be getting better and then died. You visit her in her home.

Scenario B

A man loses his twenty-one-year-old son in a drunk driving accident. It was a single car accident, so the father is having a hard time coming to terms with his son's actions. The son was in college and being coached to take over the family business. You go to the visitation at the funeral home, and the father draws you aside, eager to tell you that his son was really a good young man.

Ministry Skills:

Partnering with the Pastor

THESE TWELVE JESUS SENT OUT

It took an outsider to see that Moses, the leader of Israel, was not doing a good job of partnering with others. Moses couldn't see it for himself. Read Exodus 18:13-27. Sometimes it also takes an outsider to see if the pastor of a congregation is adequately sharing the workload with the deacons and elders and if the deacons and elders are picking up their part of the load. How would you rate your pastor at sharing this ministry given to you? How would you rate yourself at being willing to shoulder your own responsibility for this ministry?

Pray that God will remove all obstacles to being a full participant and team member in the ministry to which God has called your congregation.

SENT OUT WITH INSTRUCTIONS

Common Ministry

As congregations have increasingly developed a North American consumer mindset, congregational leadership has had to acquire a higher level of skill in many areas of ministry. When deacons/elders try to offer such skills, it soon becomes obvious that no one person is equally gifted for all areas of ministry. In 1 Corinthians 12:27-31, Paul outlines a wide variety of ministry gifts and indicates that not all are apostles, prophets, teachers, miracle workers, or healers. Not everyone can speak in tongues or interpret what has been said. It takes the entire body of Christ to do God's will on this earth.

In the same way, no one pastor can meet the needs of an entire congregation. Some will have stronger gifts in preaching but not in pastoral care. Some will be natural teachers but find administrative details frustrating. As a result many congregations now consider the elders or deacons and pastor(s) a ministry team and call upon individual elders and deacons for their ministry gifts, as well as for their spiritual health.

As this occurs, elders and deacons find they must be more deliberate about how they team with the pastor in ministry. The time is past when elders and deacons only came to meetings and gave the pastor counsel for handling situations. Now when the elders or deacons meet, everyone contributes from their own experiences of primary ministry. Even though the pastor still will provide the majority of the ministry in the congregation, elders and deacons are highly involved in actual ministry and may be authorized to carry out very specific ministries. Whom have they visited? How did it go? Who needs to be cared for? Who is following through after a mediation process for two members of the congregation?

When elders/deacons and pastors work together in this way, lay leaders understand the role of the pastor with new depth because they too have "been there and done that." This moves the congregation away from the corporate model of a governing board that hires and supervises the CEO or pastor toward a body that provides long-term spiritual vision and oversight. Even though this is a new direction and may be contrary to the way some current elders and deacons understand their role, it is a healthy move back to our Anabaptist beginnings.

Common Vision

A pastor may have a well-defined vision for the ministry of the congregation, but if the leadership team doesn't share that mission, then either overt or passive-aggressive conflict is sure to ensue. When vision for ministry or mission is established, all members of the leadership team must be willing to agree to the direction and advocate for it in the congregation.

In Anabaptist polity a unified vision for ministry is not enforced by means of a hierarchy. Rather, vision is initiated by the leadership group and adopted by the congregation. Without the entire leadership team creating and teaching this vision with a unified voice, division already has occurred and ineffectiveness is close behind. If the elders/deacons are not speaking as one, the mission is doomed to failure. In order to be faithful to God's call, we must pull together in the same direction as leaders.

Common Calling

Several distinct benefits appear when elders/deacons and pastors partner successfully. The most noticeable is that serving as an elder or deacon can be a training ground for persons trying out their call to full-time ministry. With the severe shortage of pastoral candidates in most denominations since the mid-1990s, new methods of tapping persons gifted for ministry on the shoulder have been needed. Cultivating elders and deacons who are involved in ministry is one way of calling new leadership.

Common Peace

A second benefit has been the longer tenure of pastors. Pastors who work without a leadership team often feel they are perpetually standing alone. This is because in times of conflict elders and deacons tend to side with the congregation (with whom they'll continue to share a pew long after the pastor has left) and against the pastor. This can lead to damaged congregational identity and hurtful pastoral terminations.

However, when the pastor works with elders and deacons to determine the vision for ministry and they carry it out together, they share the role of leadership. No one is left standing alone. Ministry teams that function well provide welcome stability in leadership and increased service to the congregation and community.

As You Go

Read the following example of a leadership team meeting agenda. Using situations in your own congregation, walk through a meeting as outlined.

Example of a Leadership Team Meeting Agenda

1. Check in regarding the spiritual health of each elder/deacon/pastor.

2. Report on current ministry contacts by each elder/deacon/pastor.

3. Determine ministry assignments and who is responsible for completion of each one before the next meeting.

4. Review of the mission/vision of the congregation. Are current ministries in line with what the congregation has discerned as its mission?

5. Pray for the congregation, for the needs of those providing ministry, and for those who are being ministered to.

Sources Consulted

Albright, Jim Yaussey. *Discipleship and Reconciliation Committee Handbook.* Elgin, Ill.: Brethren Press, 1995.

Arnold, Eberhard. *Why We Live in Community.* Farmington, Pa.: Plough Publishing House, 1995.

Barrett, Lois. *Doing What Is Right.* Scottdale, Pa.: Herald Press, 1989.

Bauman, Harold E. *Congregations and Their Servant Leaders.* Scottdale, Pa.: Mennonite Publishing House, 1982.

Bender, Harold S., et. al., eds. *The Mennonite Encyclopedia,* vol. 1-4. Scottdale, Pa.: Herald Press, 1955-1959.

Bender, Ross. *Education for Peoplehood.* Elkhart, Ind.: Institute for Mennonite Studies, 1997.

Blackburn, Richard and David Brubaker. "Conflict in Congregations." *In Making Peace with Conflict.* Edited by Carolyn Schrock-Shenk and Lawrence Ressler. Scottdale, Pa.: Herald Press, 1999.

Bruehl, Margaret E. "When to Call for Help," *Conciliation Quarterly* (Winter 1988): 5.

Christopher, James A. "How to Embrace Change in the Introverted Church," *Congregations* (September/October 1995): 12.

Confession of Faith in a Mennonite Perspective. Scottdale, Pa.: Herald Press, 1995.

Congregational Discipling. Scottdale, Pa.: Herald Press, 1997.

Dale, Edgar. *Audio-Visual Methods in Teaching,* 3rd ed. New York: Holt, Rinehart & Winston, 1969.

Dyck, Cornelius J., and Dennis D. Martin, eds. *The Mennonite Encyclopedia,* vol. 5. Scottdale, Pa.: Herald Press, 1990.

Epp, Frank H. *Mennonites in Canada,* 1786-1920. Toronto: Macmillan of Canada, 1974.

Groome, Thomas. *Sharing Faith*. New York: HarperCollins Publishers, 1991.

Fowler, James W. *Faith Development and Pastoral Care*. Philadelphia: Fortress Press, 1987.

Janzen, Heinz, and Dorothea Janzen. *Minister's Manual*. Newton, Kan.: Faith & Life Press and Scottdale, Pa.: Mennonite Publishing House, 1983.

Kropf, Marlene, and Kenneth Nafziger. *Singing, a Mennonite Voice*. Scottdale, Pa.: Herald Press, 2001.

Landis, Susan Mark. "Peacemaking and the Congregational Discipling Vision." In *Congregational Discipling*. Scottdale, Pa.: Herald Press, 1997.

Leadership and Authority in the Church. Scottdale, Pa.: Mennonite Publishing House, 1980.

Loewen, Howard John. *One Lord, One Church, One Hope, and One God*. Elkhart, Ind.: Institute of Mennonite Studies, 1985.

Maxwell, John C. *The 17 Essential Qualities of a Team Player*. Nashville, Tenn.: Thomas Nelson Inc., 2002.

McRae-Mahon, Dorothy. *Being Clergy, Staying Human*. Alban Institute, 1992.

Mead, Loren. *Transforming Congregations for the Future*. Alban Institute, 1994.

Mennonite Board of Congregational Ministries. *Ministerial Information Form*. Elkhart, Ind.: MBCM. Part III, 1995.

Mennonite Confession of Faith. Scottdale, Pa.: Herald Press, 1963.

Miller, Marlin E. "Some Reflections on Pastoral Ministry and Pastoral Education." In *Understanding Ministerial Leadership*. Edited by John A. Esau. Elkhart, Ind.: Institute of Mennonite Studies, 1995.

Miller, Ryan. "Turning Tangles of Tension into Knots of Strength," *Goshen College Bulletin* (September 2001): 4-5.

Noyce, Gaylord. *Church Meetings That Work*. Alban Institute, 1994.

Neuchterlein, Anne Marie. *Improving Your Multiple Staff Ministry*. Minneapolis: Augsburg Fortress, 1989.

Olsen, Charles M. "Gaining Strength from Personal Stories." In *Trust* (New Year 1996): 6-7.

———. *Transforming Church Boards into Communities of Spiritual Leaders*. Alban Institute, 1995.

Ordinal: Ministry and Ordination in the General Conference Mennonite Church, 4th draft. (GCMC Committee on the Ministry, photocopied), 1987.

Palmer, Parker. *Let Your Life Speak*. San Francisco: Jossey-Bass, 2000.

————. *The Courage to Teach: Exploring the Inner Landscape of a Teacher's Life*. San Francisco: Jossey-Bass Publishers, 1998.

Pastorate Project. *Pastor-Growing?People-Growing*. Elkhart, Ind.: Pastorate Project, 1994.

Rempel, John, ed. *Minister's Manual*. Newton, Kan.: Faith & Life Press and Scottdale, Pa.: Herald Press, 1998.

Rendle, Gil. "Congregational Revitalization." In *Inside Information*. Alban Institute, 1994.

————. "Unhooking the System," *Congregations* (July/August 1997): 15.

Shawchuck, Norman, and Roger Heuser. *Leading the Congregation*. Nashville, Tenn.: Abingdon Press, 1993.

Slough, Rebecca. "Information vs. Education," *Ohio Evangel*. Kidron, Ohio: Ohio Conference of the Mennonite Church, January 2001: 5.

Steinke, Peter. *Healthy Congregations*. Alban Institute, 1996.

————. *How Your Church Family Works*. Alban Institute, 1993.

Stoltzfus, Dale W. "Organizational Structures to Express the Congregational Discipling Vision." In *Congregational Discipling*. Scottdale, Pa.: Herald Press, 1997.

Thomas, Everett, ed. *A Mennonite Polity for Ministerial Leadership*. Newton, Kan.: Faith & Life Press, 1996.

Verduin, Leonard, tr., and J. C. Wenger, ed. *Complete Writings of Menno Simons*, c.1496-1561. Scottdale, Pa.: Herald Press, 1956.

Waltner, Erland. "A Brief Biblical/Historical Perspective." In *Called to Caregiving*. Edited by June A. Gibble and Fred W. Swartz. Elgin, Ill.: Brethren Press, 1987.

Wenger, J. C. *Introduction to Theology*. Scottdale, Pa.: Herald Press, 1954.

Wilmot, William, and Joyce Hocker. *Interpersonal Conflict*, 6th ed. New York: MacGraw Hill, 2001.

Job Description Outline for Deacons/Elders

Terms. How long is a term? How many terms may each one serve?

Appointments. How is a deacon or elder appointed? How does a deacon or elder discern whether to continue in that role?

Time Commitment. How much time is a deacon/elder to devote to fulfilling the needs of the position on a weekly basis?

Ministries of the Deacons/Elders

a. *Caring for the needy:* How is this accomplished? Who dispenses the alms fund?

b. *Pastoral Care/visitation:* How do the deacons/elders coordinate visitation?

c. *Managing conflict:* What is the accepted procedure for becoming involved in personal conflict situations in the congregation?

d. *Supporting the pastor(s):* What kind of support does the pastor request?

e. *Leadership in worship:* Are deacons or elders expected to be involved in worship? If so, in what capacities?

f. *Administration:* What are the annual administrative tasks assigned to the elders (e.g., membership questions, interviewing baptismal candidates, etc.)?

g. *Spiritual care of the congregation:* How do you test the spiritual health of the congregation? What do you do to maintain the congregation's spiritual health?

Signed by: *(all deacons/elders)*

_____

_____

_____

_____

_____

_____

_____

Dated: _____

Leadership Team Covenant for Elders/Deacons/Pastors

---

1. Spiritual Commitments to One Another
- How will the deacons/elders care for one another's spiritual life?

- How will you be accountable to each other for a healthy spiritual life?

- What do you commit to do for your own spiritual growth?

2. Deacon/Elder Meetings

- What are the expectations of the group for attendance?

- What is an acceptable reason for missing?

- How often will the deacon/elder team meet?

- How long will each meeting last?

- Who will chair the meetings?

- Who will prepare the agenda?

- How does a member of the team get an item placed on the agenda?

3. Public Decorum

- How will the team act or speak in public or with individuals if they together or individually cannot agree with an action taken by the congregation or by the pastor(s)?

4. Confidentiality

- Information is power. How will that power be shared?

- How far is information shared on the team?

- Will permission of persons involved always be sought before information is shared? Is there any circumstance in which information may be shared without permission?

- Are deacons and elders free to share information with spouses or significant others?

- Are these guidelines made known up front to individuals and to the congregation?

5. Conflict

- How will disagreements be handled?

- What outside person/resource will be used to help process conflict?

6. Complaints

- How will an individual deacon/elder receive complaints from congregational members?

- How will an individual deacon/elder receive complaints about other deacons or elders?

- To whom or where should complaints be directed?

- Will the deacon/elder group hear and respond to anonymous complaints?

- How will anonymous letters and complaints be handled?

7. Accountability
- Will you agree to be accountable to each other for your words, your actions, and your spiritual life?

8. Collaborative Way of Thinking
- What agreements can you make about how everyone will participate in group decisions, discussion, and ministry?

- Are there any times when an individual deacon or elder may speak on behalf of the entire group without first speaking to the group? If so, under what circumstances?

9. Sexuality
- Can we agree that inappropriate sexual expression has no place in our ministering relationships?

- Can we agree to be honest with each other when you see one of you spending too much time with a member of the congregation?

- Can we agree to be candid when another deacon or elder tells a joke or makes a comment or gesture that makes you uncomfortable?

- What are the physical actions, words, jokes, or personal information that you consider appropriate or inappropriate to share?

  - In the deacon/elder circle?

  - In the congregation?

- How does this affect your ministry, especially in home visitation?

10. Congregational Commitments

- In light of these agreements, overall what does the deacon/ elder team commit to the congregation (i.e., regular prayer, modeling healthy relationships, availability, etc.)?

Signed by: *(all deacons/elders)*

....

....

....

....

....

....

....

....

Dated: ....

Agreeing and Disagreeing in Love

Commitments for Mennonites in Times of Disagreement

"Making every effort to maintain the unity of the Spirit in the bond of peace," (Eph. 4:3) as both individual members and the body of Christ, we pledge that we shall:

In Thought

Accept conflict

1. Acknowledge together that conflict is a normal part of our life in the church. (Rom. 14:1-8, 10-12, 17-19; 15:1-7)

Affirm hope

2. Affirm that as God walks with us in conflict we can work through to growth. (Eph. 4:15-16)

Commit to prayer

3. Admit our needs and commit ourselves to pray for a mutually satisfactory solution (no prayers for my success or for the other to change but to find a joint way). (James 5:16)

In Action

Go to the other ...

4. Go directly to those with whom we disagree; avoid behind-the-back criticism.* (Matt. 5:23-24; 18:15-20)

In the spirit of humility ...

5. Go in gentleness, patience and humility. Place the problem between us at neither doorstep and own our part in the conflict instead of pointing out the others'. (Gal. 6:1-5)

Be quick to listen,

6. Listen carefully, summarize and check out what is heard before responding. Seek as much to understand as to be understood. (James 1:19; Prov. 18:13)

Be slow to judge,

7. Suspend judgments, avoid labeling, end name calling, discard threats, and act in a non-defensive, nonreactive way. (Rom. 2:1-4; Gal. 5:22-26)

Be willing to negotiate.

8. Work through the disagreements constructively. (Acts 15; Phil. 1-11)
   - Identify issues, interests, and needs of both (rather than take positions).
   - Generate a variety of options for meeting both parties' needs (rather than defending one's own way).
   - Evaluate options by how they meet the needs and satisfy the interests of all sides (not one side(s) values).
   - Collaborate in working out a joint solution (so both sides gain, both grow and win).
   - Cooperate with the emerging agreement

(accept the possible, not demand your ideal).

- Reward each other for each step forward, toward agreement (celebrate mutuality).

In Life

Be steadfast in love, 9. Be firm in our commitment to seek a mutual solution; be stubborn in holding to our common foundation in Christ; be steadfast in love. (Col. 3:12-15)

Be open to mediation, 10. Be open to accept skilled help. If we can not reach agreement among ourselves, we will use those with gifts and training in mediation in the larger church. (Phil. 4:1-3)

Trust the community, 11. We will trust the community and if we cannot reach agreement or experience reconciliation, we will turn the decision over to others in the congregation or from the broader church. (Acts 15)

- In one-to-one or small group disputes, this may mean allowing others to arbitrate.
- In congregational, conference district or denominational disputes, this may mean allowing others to arbitrate or implementing constitutional decision-making processes, insuring that they are done in the spirit of these guidelines, and abiding by whatever decision is made.

Be the Body of
Christ.

12. Believe in and rely on the solidarity of the Body of Christ and its commitment to peace and justice, rather than resort to the courts of law. (1 Cor. 6:1-6)

* "Go directly" if you are European-North American; in other cultures disagreements are often addressed through a trusted go-between.

From the General Conference Mennonite Church and Mennonite Church General Boards, March-April 1995. Used with permission.

NOTES

NOTES

AUTHOR

Author Anne Stuckey discovered through leading retreats for the Congregational Leadership office of the Mennonite Church that elder and deacon boards were the most maligned group in the church. High expectations were projected onto these lay leaders, she notes, yet few could articulate the ministry they were called to do. "The heartbreak of so many elders and deacons spurred me on to learn more and to write this manual to fill that need."

Anne's passion for training ministry leaders remained through cancer treatment and the completion of a doctorate in education.

She has a master of arts degree from Associated Mennonite Biblical Seminary and doctorate in education from the Graduate Theological Foundation of Indiana. Anne has been a pastor in Iowa and Ohio, and served ten years at the Mennonite Board of Congregational Ministries. She has two young adult children and is married to Terry, a physician assistant.